BEESTINGS

# BEESTINGS & BOILIE

## MEMORIES OF A NORTHUMBERLAND CHILDHOOD

### MAGGIE BARDSLEY

WITH ILLUSTRATIONS BY
### CRAIG BARDSLEY

*Barbara
best wishes

Maggie Bardsley.*

YOUCAXTON PUBLICATIONS
OXFORD & SHREWSBURY

FOR MY FAMILY

# The Toland Family as It Was During the Period of These Memoirs

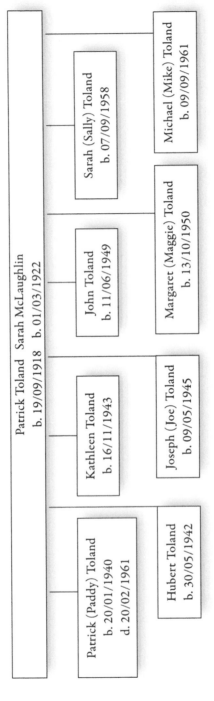

Patrick Toland   Sarah McLaughlin
b. 19/09/1918   b. 01/03/1922

Patrick (Paddy) Toland
b. 20/01/1940
d. 20/02/1961

Kathleen Toland
b. 16/11/1943

John Toland
b. 11/06/1949

Sarah (Sally) Toland
b. 07/09/1958

Hubert Toland
b. 30/05/1942

Joseph (Joe) Toland
b. 09/05/1945

Margaret (Maggie) Toland
b. 13/10/1950

Michael (Mike) Toland
b. 09/09/1961

# The Toland Family

Top Row: Joe, Kathleen, Paddy
Centre: Dad, Mum
Bottom Row: Hubert, Margaret (Me), John, Sally, Michael

# North-East Northumberland

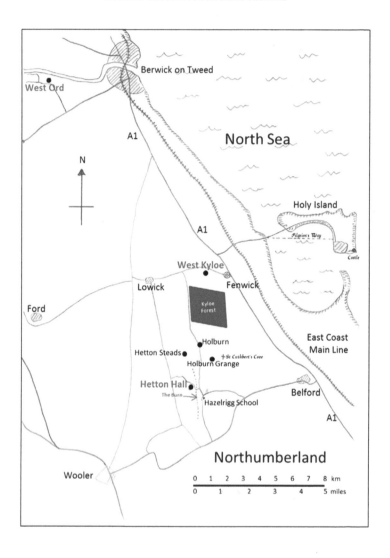

# Hetton Hall Farm

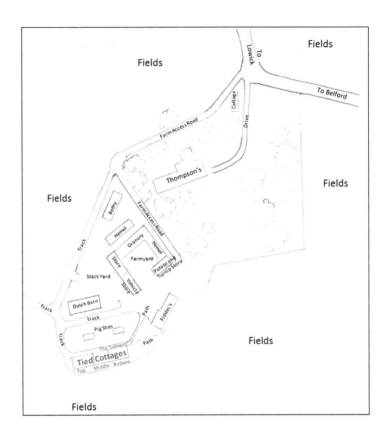

# Preface

We turn right off the Belford/Wooler road at the Hazelrigg School junction - this was my first school but in present day it is a B&B - and take the road down to Hetton Hall. It is cold but the sky is a clear blue and the sun is casting a low light over the landscape. We turn the 'dangerous' corner and head towards the burn and I am surprised to feel my throat constrict.

Now I am standing on the steps to the front door. They look like the original steps. Large chunks of cement have been chipped from the edges and they have that air of age that cannot be manufactured. The front door is painted green. The strip of cement that spans the length of the three terraced cottages is still there, except a large gate has been erected to separate our end cottage from the other two. I wonder why that is. Behind me stand the original pigsties, one sty for each cottage; they are filled with logs. The Dutch barn in the stack yard has been replaced by a row of garages. The farm sheds, cattle hemmels and granary have been converted into luxury holiday lets.

I have a curious feeling of butterflies as Mac unlocks the door and enters ahead of me. I follow and as soon as I step into the kitchen, which back then was the living room as well, my eyes cloud with tears. How wonderfully familiar this room is. I see my mother stoking the fire and my brothers and sister sitting around the table while Dad dozes in his brown leather armchair on the left of the fireplace, a mug of tea going cold on the hearth. I wipe my eyes and the vision fades.

A brand new living room has been built against the gable. It is a lovely room with large windows on two sides. The space is filled with light and the views extend across the fields toward the Belford and Chatton moors. How my parents could have used this extra space. A patio door leads to a small decking area with a wooden table and benches. I wish the weather was warmer so that I could sit here and breathe in the memories. The third bedroom at the other end of the cottage is missing. I assume it has been given over to the middle cottage to make it larger for a holiday let. The old toilet, bathroom and scullery have been converted into one large contemporary bathroom. The cottage has changed yet it still feels like my old home.

I stand at the front door and look down the slope towards the old farmyard. The new holiday cottages block the view but I can still see a path through the buildings, through the years and watch the memories flow back.

My husband Mac and I are about to spend a week here so that I can immerse myself in the environment into which I was born sixty-five years ago and spent the first ten years of my life. As I grow older I find myself frequently thinking back to childhood and feel a strong need to record the memories and stories of my own young life. How I wish I had asked my parents more about their experiences so that I could indulge in their early years. I don't want my children and grandchildren to have similar regrets, so this memoir is for them.

It is well known that memories can be unreliable so I have drawn heavily on my brother John and sister Kath, who have helped validate the truth of each chapter and who have filled in the gaps where my memory is sketchy. Parts of this chronicle are based on events before I was born so I have relied on accounts that have been handed down through the years from other relatives.

The memoir is largely chronological but it is also thematic so some chapters do move backward and forward in time.

# Contents

# Chapter 1

# Hetton Hall – The Cottages

I awoke, startled. My body was damp with sweat and my tummy hurt. Confused and afraid in the darkness I hauled myself up to sit. Before I could focus and bring myself to stand my stomach gave a violent lurch and its contents spewed over my hands, the sheets and my nightclothes. Dazed, I sat still a few moments unsure of what had just happened. In a state of shock and terror I recovered my voice and yelled, "Mammy, Mammy."

No one responded.

I screamed, "Mammy, Mammy."

Where was my mammy? I began to sob. Tears spilled into my lap and as I wiped my eyes vomit smeared across my cheeks. Where was everyone? Where were my mammy and daddy? Where were my brothers and sister? Why would no one help me?

"Mammy!"

Without understanding why, I suddenly became calm and settled, as if I'd been lowered into a warm bath. I sensed a presence and glanced up. Before me floated the 'man in the moon' outside the bedroom window. His round yellow body tapered to a point like a balloon and it filled the window frame. His large, soulful eyes bathed me in kindness as he hovered. He spun moonbeams across the room and wrapped me in a soft moonbeam blanket. Through a blur of tears

I returned his gaze, transfixed and full of wonderment, comforted more than I knew why. The 'man in the moon' began to move and before I could call out to him, "please stay", he floated up and away and out of sight.

That was my first memory. I had been asleep in a cot in Mum and Dad's bedroom. How I wished for a proper bed, after all I was three years old. Why must I still sleep like a baby? My older brothers and sister shared the beds in the other bedroom; there was no room for me.

My parents had been next door making merry with the neighbours. The adults seldom had time to socialise. Occasionally they gathered in one another's houses to celebrate some event and would leave older children in charge of the little ones. As for me being in the charge of my siblings, either they were asleep or they chose to ignore me. It seemed impossible they could sleep through my screams.

My mother smiled when I told her about the man in the moon. She said it had just been a dream. My brothers scoffed and called me "Stupid." If they had played a trick on me they never owned up. I prefer to think of it as my own special 'man in the moon' visitation.

I was born in the middle cottage of a row of three modest, whitewashed, single storied tied cottages on Hetton Hall farm. Hetton Hall is a few miles southwest of Berwick-on-Tweed in Northumberland. My mother went into labour on Friday 13th October 1950. The autumn leaves lay scattered on the 'Cement', a stretch of concrete that spanned the length of the cottages. The first hints of a crisp winter were already in the air. My poor mother prayed to God I would at least be patient until after mid-night to avoid a 'Black Friday' birth, but her prayers went the way of all prayers and I emerged in the evening of that cursed day. As she watched me grow and glide into adulthood her superstition subsided, because my life was neither blighted nor unlucky.

I was another mouth to feed though. My entry into the family made the count six. Paddy came first and then within a seven year period Mum gave birth to four more children; Hubert, Kathleen, Joe and John. Sixteen months on from John and ten years since Paddy, I joined the brood. As soon as transport could be arranged several weeks later, my parents took me to the Catholic Church in the village of Lowick to be christened Margaret Mary Toland.

Soon after my christening we moved from the middle cottage to the larger top end cottage. This consisted of a living room, a scullery, a bathroom and toilet, and two slightly bigger bedrooms. The humble living room was the hub of the cottage, where the cooking, eating and relaxing took place. A fire burned in the grate throughout the year, throwing out waves of heat. Through the bitter winter months we struggled to become fully warm. The fire's heat fought a losing battle against the icy drafts, which crept under the doors and through the single paned window. During those months we huddled around the fire, each trying to push closer than the other. Our faces glowed pink and our body fronts sweltered from the flames but we shivered as icy tentacles crept down our backs. Tilley lamp and candlelight shadows flickered about the room at night.[1] In sharp contrast to the living room the bedrooms were arctic. Each night we put on our pyjamas in front of the fire and then took as few leaps as possible to travel along the corridor and jump into bed. We snuggled together and clutched the hot water bottles Mum had already placed beneath the blankets.

The fire range had an integrated oven to the right hand side and two hinged circular wrought iron pan holders, one either side of the grate, that could swivel over the flames. My mother cooked over the fire. I can still see her hunched over the long-handled saucepans, blackened on the outside from coal soot, testing with a fork to see if the food was cooked. Usually a large pan of potatoes bubbled away on one of the holders while a kettle rested on the other. Potatoes and tea - those were our staples. If we were lucky Mum might put soda bread in the oven; if we were luckier still she would bake a rice pudding. Each morning, while we slumbered, she got up and set the fire. Until the flames were blazing there would be no tea. Dad, already out in the fields, would be in soon for breakfast; the kettleful of water must be boiling and waiting.

Cottage life was cramped, privacy at a premium. My mother possessed a deep well of patience but when we children bickered the noise filled every space and drove her to distraction. Dad would be out at work on the farm but she had no escape.

"Glory be to God, will yous get out of my road," she would say, her soft Irish accent trailing behind as she shooed us outside to play. At other times she threatened, "You wait until your Father gets home."

---

1 The luxury of electricity was a few years into the future.

Fear of our father usually stopped the fights. Despite the threats she never did tell on us. She knew Dad too well. He would take off his belt at the slightest provocation and give us a sound thrashing. How we trembled as we watched him undo his buckle and slip his belt through his trouser loops. When the belt did come off, Paddy and Hubert took the worst of the beating. They were older, they should know better.

Of the three cottages my mother coveted the one at the bottom end, which had three bedrooms and a slightly larger living room. When news came the property would soon become vacant my parents staked their claim to it. The Drums, the current occupants, would move out in a few weeks, "and the sooner the better", I heard my dad say. "A right rough lot all right," my mum returned. The eight unkempt Drum children led my brothers and sister astray. Davy Drum owned an air rifle, which he fired indiscriminately at birds and rabbits, but on occasion the rifle pointed at us children. It's a wonder none of us was ever hurt.

Yet my sister and older brothers spent many hours playing with the Drums. Kathleen recounted a particular game of cowboys and indians that frightened her so much the memory has stayed with her. She and Maureen Drum had pleaded to be the cowboys for a change. The boys relented but before the two girls had time to draw their pistols the boys captured them and tied them to a totem pole. Davy Drum set firewood beneath the pole and told them they were to be burnt alive. The girls were convinced he meant what he said - he was crazy enough to do so. Despite their struggles they could not free themselves from their bindings and became terrified. Kathleen and Maureen's screams and wails brought the mothers running, thinking someone had been murdered in the hay barn.

The Drums moved on to another farm and we never saw nor heard of them again.

I was four when we moved into the bottom end cottage. My mother was delighted with the extra space and I shifted from the cot in their room to share a bedroom with Kathleen.

The bottom cottage is the one I remember the most. Furnishings were sparse; a dresser stood against the sidewall. Two brown leather armchairs were placed either side of the fire, one for Dad and the other for Mum. A matching two-seater couch was positioned between them in front of the fire. A table, covered with a pale green oilcloth, patterned with tiny white and yellow flowers, was pushed up against the back wall and four chairs tucked beneath. Rag rugs, which Mum and Kathleen fashioned from old clothing scraps, offered soft areas and warmth against the stone floor. A green picture rail ran across every wall approximately a foot from the ceiling. A large picture of Jesus Christ hung on this rail above the fireplace. His brown hair fell in waves around his shoulders.

"Our protector," my mother said.

To me, his presence threatened. No matter where I stood in the room his eyes followed me, assessing and judging. I disliked this picture intensely and even though his face wore a gentle expression, pitying even, and his delicate hands held wide in peace, it was his exposed heart that dripped beads of dark red blood that disturbed me the most.

Regardless of this ever-present menace the small room was my sanctuary. Here, alone with my mother while the others were at school, I could squeeze out every bit of her love without having to share. But this exquisite attention could never last. Soon I too was sent to school. Pre-schools were non-existent in those days for me to become used to the idea. So, despite the excitement of being all grown up enough to learn, I was as nervous as a kitten on my first day.

John held me by the hand as we walked into the playground. Twenty or more children ran backwards and forwards and whooped and bellowed in high-pitched tones. I clung to John afraid and feeling trapped when a few boys encircled us. Curious, beady eyes peered into my face and poked at my clothes.

Surrounded by his playmates John tried to shrug me off but I clung to him like a limpet. At last Mrs Wright, the infants teacher and wife to the headmaster, ushered me to a girl called Anne Steel who had short fair hair and wore a green and white gingham dress. Mrs Wright said Anne would look after me and show me what to do. I was unsure whether I liked this girl; she didn't smile and refused to hold my hand. Rather she treated me, the new girl, as an unwanted chore, an unfair punishment. I stayed close to her all the same.

Within a week I too ran around the playground happier than I thought possible. I had given up on Anne Steel and had become friends with the headmaster's daughter, Ann Wright. We remained friends until the day I left the school forever.

John and I had hair of the whitest blonde; mine a bundle of curls, which my mother tugged at with the hairbrush into a ponytail away from my eyes. I cried every morning when she yanked out the tats, which had developed overnight.

"Will yer stop yer crying? It will be over soon."

I knew better and would jerk my head away from the brush in rebellious remonstrations. I suffered the pain until every knot had been smoothed. Even then I could not escape until several ringlets, formed by Mum curling chunks of my ponytail around her middle finger, bounced like lambs tails in spring. She loved my hair and felt proud when people stopped and said, "Eee, your wee lass has such bonny blonde curls." I threatened to take the scissors and cut it all off. [2]

As she hurried John and me out of the cottage for school, our mother would stand at the door and trace our journey. She looked out for our two blonde heads bobbing in time with each other as we ran across the field towards the burn until we were beyond the hill and out of sight. She would pick us out again as we ran along the road to the 'dangerous'

---

2 Many years later I did just that, to within half an inch from my scalp.

corner where we disappeared from view. When she saw our white heads cross the stile that led up to the school she knew we were safely around the corner. Then she would relax and turn to her daily chores.

The school, situated on a rise a little over a mile away, could be seen from our cottage. To a four year old, the distance seemed a hundred miles and I felt sure my legs could never carry me that far. My older brothers and sister had left the house earlier and walked to the road end to catch the school bus that took them to the secondary modern at Wooler, ten miles away.

I could hardly wait until I was old enough to ride on that bus.

# Chapter 2

# Emigration

My parents originated from County Donegal, Ireland. They lived close by the rugged but beautiful shores of Malin Head on the Inishowen peninsular, which juts out to the North Atlantic Ocean. Malin Head is the most northerly point in Ireland where fierce wind and rainstorms can rage for days. The remoteness and dangerous waters around the coast prompted a weather station to be established there in the 1950s. To this day reports of the local weather are sent to the BBC for the daily Shipping Forecasts.

Malin Head is made up of a number of small communities of which three are relevant to this story; Ballygorman, Killourt and five miles inland, the Glen, which for some unfathomable reason, the locals call the Black Mountain. The population is overwhelmingly Roman Catholic and, in my parents' day, families were large. My mother was one of ten children and my father one of thirteen. At that time the area was relatively isolated and inbreeding within communities was an issue. To lessen the problem marriages were encouraged across communities. In particular, the men from the Black Mountain were renowned for their 'raids' on the other two communities when they would entice the local girls to a life in the hills. Dad, a Toland from Ballygorman wooed and married Mum, a McLaughlin from Killourt.

Fishing was the main employment. After he left school at fourteen my father, like many other young men in the area, had no choice but to find work on the fishing boats. This meant long hard hours in stormy, ferocious waters. No wonder that in 1946 he leapt at the opportunity to leave the boats behind and start a different life across the Irish Sea.

At the end of the Second World War English landowners sent agents to Ireland to recruit men to address the shortfall in farm workers. This was the opportunity that presented itself to Dad. He judged that farm labouring would surely be more lucrative than fishing, and better enable him to provide for his wife and, at that time, four children. John and I were not yet born.

In May 1946 Dad left his family behind and took a job on a farm as a labourer at West Ord near Berwick-on-Tweed, Northumberland. The farm stood high on the banks of the River Tweed, which forms the border between England and Scotland. He had intended to work for a few months until he had enough money to secure one of the farm's tied cottages, after which his family would join him. Until then he lodged in a bothy. He knew about bothies and had expected to share with other itinerant workers, but what a shock when he found he had to live with men who were rough and filthy in their habits. My dad was no 'softie', and while only a small man, he was as tough as any, but he had to tolerate men who cared little for personal hygiene, who smelled of urine and rarely washed. He found it an uncomfortable way to live, worse even than the fishing boats. No wonder he was determined to move out as soon as possible.

Two years would pass before he saw his family again.

Meanwhile, Mum existed on the scant money Dad posted to her each week. By the time he paid his lodging, food and beer, the latter a necessity, otherwise he might 'die of the thirst' he said, his wages had dwindled. Mum struggled to feed and clothe four children. Arguably though, she had the better deal because she had the love and support of her parents and brothers and sisters, who lived nearby. If the truth be told she would just as soon stay in her beloved Malin Head - the very best place in the world to live, she said, and continued to say to the end of her days. My father found it hard to be separated from his family. Two years was a long time out of the bonding process and this may have contributed to the harshness with which he later treated his children.

After two years had passed, Dad travelled to Malin Head to bring his family back to England with him. However, due to a problem with her birth certificate, Mum had not yet received her passport - without which she would unable to make the trip to England. Dad was unaware of this problem and she had no way to contact him to warn him to delay his trip. Each day she expected her passport to be delivered but the postal service was slow and unpredictable. Dad arrived as planned and I can hear his angry words and agitation at the discovery of the missing passport.

"Jesus Sadie, I cannut afford to waste good money to come over all this way and you not come back with me."

On the day of the family's planned departure Mum's passport had still not arrived. She was unable to travel. Dad would have raged. He would lose his job if he delayed his journey. He had no choice but to return to England and once again, leave his family behind.

When Mum's passport did finally arrive she no longer had an excuse to stay in Malin Head. She was twenty-three years old and in all that time had ventured no further than the Black Mountain. In a few days she would leave her home and travel three hundred miles to the other side of England. As each day passed her natural happy demeanour changed to one of growing sorrow and anxiety.

"God knows I might never see home again."

Mum was forced to make the trip to England without Dad's help - he could not afford to return to Malin Head. In many ways my mother was a fearful person. Her life in Malin Head had been rustic and simple - hard working with few luxuries. In this remote area, cut off from the mainstream, she had been protected from the outside world and modern life. She had no desire to live anywhere else and must have been terrified at the thought of the journey to a strange land. She would be on her own, with luggage and four children under the age of eight, and Joe only a toddler. I could imagine her torment, wrenched from everything she knew and loved.

The plan was for Mum and her children to travel as third class passengers on the cattle boat from Londonderry port to Glasgow. From there they would catch a bus to Berwick-upon-Tweed where Dad would meet them.

The day of departure must have been agonising. I can imagine Mum clinging to her parents, tearful, sobbing, forcing herself with every ounce of her will to board the bus that would take her away from Malin Head and on to Londonderry. I picture her turn in her seat and look back, through a film of tears, at the feeble waves from her mother and father. She would sit in this position until the bus rounded the corner and she lost sight of her family.

Ahead lay the long road to Londonderry and an unknown life. Her older brother Mickey travelled with her as far as the port to help with the luggage and the children – at least she could take comfort from his company.

Mum had heard stories about these cattle boats. An area in the boat's belly close to the cattle was segregated as third class accommodation. Rows of rough, wooden slats served as seats and beds. The smell from the cattle and stench from other traveller's vomit would have been noxious and intolerable. My mother, brothers and sister would have endured the discomfort and Mum would have struggled to control her own nausea.[3]

At the port the family walked towards the passenger gangplank. The low of cattle hummed against a backdrop of slaps and male shouts of "Get up there," as the animals were urged to step onto an adjacent gangplank. Mickey placed the luggage on the ground. From this point Mum was forced to manage by herself or rely on strangers to help. She picked up Joe with one arm and hurried the older children up the gangplank. When she lifted the heavy suitcase with her free hand she stumbled on the bottom rung.

Alarmed, Mickey said, "Sadie, you cannut possibly manage four wee 'uns and that suitcase on your own. You just cannut do it. You have to find the bus at the other end. How are you going to do that and carry the babby, and the suitcase, and mind the wee 'uns?

"Give me the babby," he said.

---

3 She had never been a comfortable traveller and I remember, on many occasions in future years, when I had to stop the car for her.

Mum pulled Joe closer to her and shook her head in disbelief. No way would she give up her child.

"Mammy and Daddy and Rosie will look after him. You can come home and fetch him next year. Come on now, give me the babby."

Mum's older sister Rosie was unmarried and without children of her own. She had devoted much of her time to Joe and had helped Mum with the little ones while Dad was away.

Concerned for his younger sister's welfare and the ordeal that lay ahead, Mickey did what he thought best and urged her, bullied even, to give up her child.

How Mum must have sobbed as she handed Joe to Mickey. Sometimes life's choices are just too difficult. If her passport had arrived in time Dad would have been with her to help with the children and luggage. She would not have been forced into this choice. I never discussed this dilemma with her. She felt guilty and tormented enough without being reminded.[4]

Mum was one of the youngest in her family and was well used to '*doing as she was told*'. Against all her motherly instincts she '*did as she was told*'.

The boat sailed up the Foyle River into Loch Foyle and then out into the Atlantic Ocean. There followed an overnight trip through rough winter seas, until the boat entered the calmer waters of the River Clyde and on into Glasgow port.

In January 1948, Mum stepped off that boat into a new life with only three of her children by her side.

Five years and two more children would elapse before she saw her babby again.[5]

---

[4] I've often wondered how long she resisted before she finally realised perhaps she couldn't manage. I've also wondered, if in her place at that time, what choice would I have made? I'm grateful not to have ever been put in such a position. With our affluence and easy forms of communication, how can we possibly know what our own reaction would have been in the same circumstances?

[5] A year later Dad returned to Malin Head to bring Joe home. By this time Rosie, Granny and Granda had grown very fond of him and were reluctant to give him up, which in turn may have influenced the three-year-old boy. He refused to leave. Dad returned to England, once more without him.

# Chapter 3

# West Ord

The cottage in West Ord was tiny, smaller even than the home my parents left behind in Malin Head. The single storey dwelling consisted of a bedroom, a living room and a scullery no bigger than a cupboard. The lavatory or midden was outside. The children slept in the attic on mattresses laid on the floor and each night Mum lowered the attic ladder so Paddy, Hubert and Kathleen could climb to bed.

Tilley lamps and candles provided dim light. The cottage lacked plumbing therefore Paddy and Hubert fetched buckets of water from the farmyard pump. Lugging heavy buckets was a chore hence water was used sparingly. Fewer cups of tea for Mum and fewer tin baths for all. Once a week, in front of the fire, Mum filled the tin bath with several kettles full of hot water and then topped up with cold; all the children shared this single bath of water. They argued about who bathed first, each determined to avoid stepping into cooler, dirtier water. None of this would have been unfamiliar to my parents because the facilities back home in Ireland had been similar.

The cottage stood in a lovely spot high on the banks of the River Tweed, three miles west of the historic town of Berwick-upon-Tweed. Sand martins flitted in and out of their nesting holes in the sand banks as they fed on the insects above the water. On the other side of the river the Scottish borderlands stretched far and beyond. Life had been difficult but at least my parents had moved to tranquil countryside.

Soon after Mum arrived in West Ord snow began to fall and during that winter, it fell heavily. Strong winds caused high drifts, which cut the farm off from the main roads. Mum must have wondered 'what in God's name have I moved to'. She and the children had no experience of such thick snow. It rarely snowed in Malin Head due to the salt-laden atmosphere. Here it had banked up against the front door and Dad had to dig a way out. At least now they didn't need to go far to fetch water. How much easier to drag in buckets of snow than to trudge to the well?

When the thaw came, it came quickly and caused a rapid melt. The ground became saturated and the surplus water from the surrounding countryside needed an outlet. By some unlucky feature of the land the water coursed across the road and, to my parent's dismay, flowed into the cottage. Mum threw her hands to her mouth and groaned, "Jesus, what have I done to deserve this." She believed if bad things happened to you then you must have been bad. "God finds his own ways to punish you."

She and Dad hoisted what little furniture they could into the attic and, during the few days of the flood, they too climbed the ladder and slept with the children among the displaced table and chairs. Conditions must have been confined indeed but better that than have their meagre possessions ruined. The snow and floods eventually subsided; the family settled back into their new home and quickly became part of the farm community.

Some time later, Hubert, a soon to be six-year-old, snaffled a pair of scissors and persuaded Kathleen to let him cut her hair. She dutifully stood still while he snipped at her curls. Her locks fell to the floor in uneven chunks; snip after snip, until Hubert had satisfied himself the job was done. My mother screeched when she saw the result. She did her best to trim and tidy the uneven tufts but the bald patches were impossible to hide. "Jesus, Mary and Joseph, the shame of it. What will the neighbours think," she said. Rather than display her daughter's unusual haircut to the world Mum forced Kathleen to wear a pink pixie hat whenever she went out. When they were invited into the neighbours' houses for tea and a gossip Mum ordered Kathleen to keep the hat on throughout. Her shame didn't stretch to how odd that must have seemed. Poor Kathleen, she came to hate that hat with its dangling tassels tied beneath her chin. Once her hair had grown to a respectable length the hat was cast into the bin, never to be worn again. It would be a long time before Hubert persuaded her into other misdeeds.

Whilst Mum missed Ireland desperately she found the people from the North East friendly and always willing to lend a hand. Mr Clarke, the landowner was particularly sympathetic and generous. He lived in the 'Big House' associated with the farm. The house stood grand and white against a backdrop of low farm buildings. Mr Clarke was affluent by farm workers' standards and on occasion he would attend auctions to buy second-hand furniture, which he then sold to the farm workers at a price much less than he paid. Mr Clarke's benevolence meant the workers could furnish their cottages with much better quality items than they could ever otherwise have afforded. Indeed some of those pieces may now be valuable antiques.

Another example of the community's humanity was the compassion they showed to a tramp, who trudged into the farm on a regular basis. They humoured his strange habits, gave him a bite to eat and let him sleep in the hay barn. This old eccentric would scrounge newspapers from the labourers and, when he took himself off to sleep for the night, would undress 'buck naked' and cover his body with the newspapers as blankets. The children sniggered behind their hands at the funny old man and would peek into the barn hoping to catch a glimpse of his bare bottom. When Mum discovered what they were up to she threatened, "I'll tan yer hides so I will, if I catch yous doing that again."

In return for the hospitality the vagrant would pick a few potatoes or clean out a shed until such time as he became bored and trudged on to the next obliging community.

In early spring 1948 the postman delivered a telegram. Dad was out working on the farm. Mum's hands trembled as she opened the envelope; telegrams usually held bad news. This one was no exception. She read the clipped words, 'Mother died. Sudden. Heart attack.' Her beautiful, angelic mother, Granny – this couldn't be true. Her howling wail brought the children to her side. Never before had they heard such a mournful cry from their mother. They huddled around her, afraid, unsure how to console her. Mum desperately needed the comfort of her father and brothers and sisters but she was three hundred miles from home and knew it would be impossible for her return to attend Granny's funeral.

The sorrow and heartache at the loss of Granny caused Mum to sink into a prolonged grief. Her health suffered. She experienced pain in her gums. They swelled and turned purple. Extra spaces appeared between her teeth and pus oozed from within. She thought the problem would improve and did nothing about it until the condition worsened causing her teeth to become loose. The doctor told her the only option was to have them all removed. She was suffering from pyorrhea, which damaged the soft tissue and bone that supported her teeth.

She returned from the dentist in a state of distress. She sat with her head over a basin and spat blood that continuously dribbled from her gaping mouth, devoid of teeth. The children snuggled together; frightened. This woman was not their mother; she was a witch with a toothless sunken jaw. They dared not approach. The day she smiled her false teeth smile the children jumped with delight. Their real mother had returned to them at last.

In early August that year the sun disappeared. Thick dark clouds brought a gloom across the county, as if the world's end was near. Rain fell and continued to fall for two weeks - four inches in the first week and another four in the second.

The River Tweed and its tributaries burst their banks causing major floods throughout the border country. Harvests were ruined and landslips and collapsed bridges caused severe disruption to road and rail systems. The Great North railway from London to Edinburgh was forced to close north of the border. The River Tweed rose to twice its volume and burst its banks in many places along its course. Mum and Dad were alarmed at the rising water and feared for their property, remembering the previous winter floods. But the high banks and wide basin at West Ord prevented the river from spilling over into the farm. While the ground did become saturated from the incessant downfall, this time the cottages were spared the floods.

The community buzzed. The locals, my parents included, gathered along the riverbank and gaped in awe at the Tweed's deluge.

"Look at thon mess in the water," someone said.

"Eee, de ye see that. It's a fishing shiel swept reet off its base," said another. The small hut used as shelter by fishermen floated downstream like a rowing boat free of its moorings.

Uprooted trees, dead animals and other debris floated past. Swans manoeuvred the flotsam as they glided by. The debris gathered momentum as it drifted downstream and, when it reached the railway viaduct in Berwick, piled up against the massive stone piers supporting the bridge. This damming prevented the river from flowing out to sea and caused four million gallons of water to pool behind the structure. The authorities feared the pressure of the wreckage would put too much strain on the viaduct and cause the whole thing to come crashing down.

The viaduct survived the tension but other damages amounted to many thousands of pounds prompting the government to set up a National Fund to help the flood victims. King George VI and Queen Elizabeth contributed.

By September the flood destruction had been cleared. My mother fell pregnant and John was born in hospital in Berwick on June 11th 1949. Seven months later she was pregnant again with me.

"Here we go again," I hear her say.

The plight of the Catholic wife: a child every eighteen months, more or less. As soon as she stopped breast-feeding one child she fell pregnant with the next. Hers was a life of heavy breasts, swollen ankles and varicose veins followed by a trail of little ones who wailed and tugged at her skirts. She will have been thankful for the pregnancy free years when she and Dad had been separated by distance. My mother loved all her children but I know she despaired each time she 'fell'.

Clearly the cottage was too small for such a growing family. Dad needed to find other work with bigger tied accommodation. In April 1950 a job became vacant on a farm owned by the Co-Operative Wholesale Society (CWS) at Hetton Hall, fifteen miles south of West Ord. Dad applied and got the job. They were to move in May and Dad delighted Mum when he told her, "The house has running water and an inside lavvy."

May was traditionally the month to move; winter was over and spring brought new beginnings. People generally moved on a Friday, which they called 'Flit Friday', an old northern saying. They thought it bad luck to flit on a Saturday; 'Saturday flit's a short sit', the saying continued. Mum would have been aware of the term and didn't like to take chances. Dad would have said, "Divn't be so stupid woman. That's superstitious baloney". I don't know if it was a Friday or a Saturday, or some other day when they packed up their belongings, but it was the first time since she had moved to this country that my mother looked forward to the change.

The cost of a removal company was beyond my parents' means; their few possessions hardly warranted one. Neither did they own a car. Instead they borrowed a tractor and trailer to move their few items of furniture from West Ord to Hetton Hall. When the trailer was packed, furniture covered in sacking and tied down to prevent it from slipping on the bumpy roads, they closed the cottage door for the last time and waved goodbye to West Ord.

Dad sat in the driver's seat of the grey Massey Ferguson - with no protective cab. The children and Mum, with John on her lap, sat on the trailer amongst the furniture. The tractor chugged slow miles along the narrow country lanes. It took the best part of an hour to drive the fifteen miles to Hetton Hall. The fresh colours of spring blossom, the purple blooms of invading rhododendrons, the cowslips and buttercups that scattered the meadows did little to take Mum's mind off the discomfort of her makeshift seat, or of her growing pregnancy bump. Paddy and Hubert chattered loudly to make themselves heard above the noise of the tractor's engine. They fooled about and pushed one another from side to side making Mum more and more nervous. As the journey stretched out the boys became restless and bored.

At last they approached the entrance road to Hetton Hall. Dad said, "Not far now, it's just around the corner." The boredom quickly changed to a state of anticipation.

The tractor was about to deliver the family to a different and exciting life.

# Chapter 4

# The Fiddeses

After the long bumpy tractor ride from West Ord my family drove into the farmyard of Hetton Hall. Big John Fiddes, the farm steward, greeted them and presented Dad with the keys to the middle cottage of the row of three terraces. The Fiddes family lived in a larger detached cottage down the slope from ours. Theirs was built of grey stone, had three bedrooms and an integral stone garage, which they used for storage.

Paddy and Hubert ran through our cottage and explored each tiny room, excited they would no longer have to climb the ladder at night to sleep in the attic. Here was a proper bedroom.

"Reet posh," they said.

They turned on the taps in the bathroom and pulled the toilet chain, mesmerised by the sound of the water as it swirled and flushed.

"Hey Mam, come and look at the water coming oot o' the taps, and there's a massive white bath in here an'all."

"Will yous stop running the water," Mum shouted. She was so used to conserving the utility and thought it a crime to let it run and not use it. "It's a terrible waste."

Despite yelling at the boys, she too marvelled at the running water and thought how much easier her life would be now.

After they had unloaded the furniture and unpacked their suitcases they settled into their new house in front of the coal fire, tired and ready for bed. The very next day Dad would be up early and out to the fields before breakfast.

The following morning Jessie Fiddes, Big John's wife, waddled up the slope and introduced herself. She was heavily pregnant with her first child. She looked at Mum's belly and said, "We'll have a lot to talk about, you and me lass."

Little did Mum know this was a foretaste of her future relationship with Jessie, for Jessie loved to natter and not a day would pass without her familiar call at our front door, "Hello, anybody in." Many a time Mum would say in exasperation, "Does that woman have no work to do?" Jessie was a good soul though and made Mum feel welcome and accepted.

In June 1950, Jessie went into labour and gave birth to a girl in the hospital at Berwick-upon-Tweed. In honour of the month they named their daughter June. Four months later, in October, I was born. After six children the novelty of a baby in our house had worn off long ago, but for Jessie and Big John, their daughter June was a precious thing indeed. She was their little darling and was spoiled accordingly.

Despite Jessie's busybody nature she and Mum became friends. They both had new daughters to care for. They consoled one another when either of them had a sleepless night, and Mum, who already had five other children, offered plenty of parenting advice when Jessie struggled.

Jessie was five foot three, verging on the plump side. She was a few years younger than Mum but already had strong wisps of grey that contrasted starkly with her dark brown hair. A noticeable moustache in the same dark colour spread across her upper lip, which John and I sniggered over in the cruel way of children. She was a nosy parker and a persistent gossip, snippets of which she picked up from conversations on the telephone. As stewards the Fiddeses were privileged to own a telephone. This black Bakelite contraption fascinated me. I thought it magic that people could talk to one another through it and I would hang around hoping to hear it ring. Sometimes I picked up the receiver when no one was watching and held pretend conversations.

Bursting to tell her pieces of news, Jessie would speed up the slope to repeat (and embellish) them to Mum. Jessie was harmless and had many good qualities and skills, such as baking. She enjoyed baking and was generous in her offerings, something my own mother rarely had the time or the inclination for. On baking days I could be found sitting in the Fiddeses kitchen licking bowls and munching on fairy cakes and shortbread biscuits.

Big John, a commanding six-foot figure with thick chocolate brown wavy hair, was responsible for managing the work of the farm labourers. He was handsome with deep-set brown eyes and a wide mouth with thick lips. He smiled a lot displaying the whitest teeth I had ever seen. He had a gentle nature and was kind to us children on whom he played silly tricks that would make us laugh. He didn't shout at or smack his own children and many a time I wished he were my dad. What a terrible admission to make but I suppose my young self felt that way. Dad chastised us often and, when we were very naughty, would beat us with his belt. John and I were younger and spared the worst of his anger, though at the time it seemed we were constantly wary of his mood.

Despite his fiery nature Dad also loved us in his own way. Many a time he would sit me on his knee after he came in from a hard day's labour and bounce me up and down while he sang a ditty that made me chuckle. My favourite was 'Brian O'Lynn'. I thought it slightly outrageous and verging on the blasphemous. He would sing...

> *Brian O'Lynn and his wife and wife's mother,*
> *They all went out to church together,*
> *The church door was locked and they couldn't get in,*
> *"We'll pray to the divvil," says Brian O'Lynn,*
> *"It'll do, yes it'll do,"*
> *Says Brian O'Lynn, "It'll do."*

> *Brian O'Lynn and his wife and wife's mother,*
> *They all went under the bridge to piddle together,*
> *One piddled needles and one piddled pins,*
> *"That's mighty sharp piddling," says Bryan O'Lynn.*
> *"It'll do, yes it'll do,"*
> *Says Brian O'Lynn, "It'll do."*

Sometimes Dad replaced the word 'piddle' with 's**t', which sent John and me into a paroxysm of giggles. Mum tutted in the background and shook her head in disapproval, but she didn't mind really. At other times Dad played his button-keyed accordion and sang Irish folk songs, his foot stamping along to the rhythm of the music. He had a good singing voice.

I never heard Big John sing to his children and he certainly didn't play the accordion. He was the farm steward and as such was subject to sneers and scorn from my dad and the other workers, but his broad shoulders shrugged off the insults. He was the farm steward and expected as much.

As June Fiddes and I grew from babies to toddlers to young girls, we too became friends - like our mothers. My first memory of our friendship was when we were three years old. We liked to play in a sandpit and I can remember a particular day when we were both totally absorbed nothing could interrupt the building of our sand sculptures, not even toilet needs. We each hunkered at the pit edge, knickers filled with pee and poo. Eventually my mother appeared, picked me up by my armpits and dragged me home scolding about being old enough to know better. Jessie could be heard scolding June in the same vein as she dragged her home

June and I were friends but, as is the way with young fickle girls, so too were we enemies. Our friendship hung suspended on a flimsy thread, which from time-to-time snapped. Like the day I challenged her to climb the narrow stone wall at the side of her house. The top of the wall had rough uneven stones on which it was hard to balance. June had always been timid and refused to join me. I kept my balance and teetered, one foot in front of the other. I don't know if it was jealousy or sheer spitefulness, but June came to the verge at the base of the wall below me, stretched up and pushed me hard. I landed in a huge nettle patch on the other side of the wall. My mother dabbed the stings that covered my body with calamine lotion to soothe the prickly burning. June denied she had pushed me and, for a time, I stayed away from her, wounded by her lie. After a few days we were back together gathering wild flowers for pressing, the nettle stings healed and forgotten.

June's dark hair hung thick and wavy. Her features and bone structure promised beauty in later years. For as long as I can remember she sucked her right hand forefinger by pushing it into the roof of her mouth and pulling it forward towards her upper front jaw. Her mother threatened, "If you don't stop that your teeth will stick out," but her pink shrivelled finger, constantly wet, remained firmly inside her mouth. Her milk teeth fell out and as her two front adult teeth grew, sure enough they stuck out, bucked like a donkey's hind legs, compromising that promised beauty.

Jessie gave birth to her son, Little John, in 1952. He was eighteen months younger and often a nuisance to us girls. One day June and I sat under the covers of her bed looking through a book. A stool, littered with drawings, was placed beside the bed. Suddenly June turned to me with a look of sheer terror.

She squeaked, "That stool just moved by itsel'."

"Don't be daft, how could it," I replied.

"It did so. You watch."

We grasped each other's hands and stared at the stool. When it nudged forward a couple of notches, clearly by itself, a chill swept through my body. A 'bogeyman' was under the bed! But Mum told me bogeymen didn't exist. I looked at June, she looked at me and we both began to scream.

"Mam, Mam!"

"Jessie, Jessie!"

Moments later Little John emerged from beneath the bed chuckling, "Haha, that scared you didn't it."

He often tried to muscle in and spoil our games. After the bed episode I had little to do with him.

Jessie gave birth to another son, Ashley, three years later – he was her last child.

The Fiddeses were the first on the farm to rent a television. I had heard rumours about the magic of TV from others at school and was delighted when Jessie allowed me and other farm children to sit on their living room floor and watch programmes such as 'My Friend Flicka', 'Lassie' or the 'Lone Ranger'. The tiny screen, encased in a dark wooden frame with two tuning knobs, flashed black and white images of horses galloping through canyons throwing up dust, while cowboys fired guns and Indians fired arrows.

I was spellbound.

The Fiddeses featured large in my young life and of all the experiences we shared over the years these are the memories that stand out.

# Chapter 5

# Hetton Hall – the Farm

The CWS farm estate was collectively known as the 'Hettons' and consisted of the following individual farms: Hetton Hall, Hetton Law, Hetton Steads, North Hazelrigg, Holborn Grange and Wrangham.

The land around Hetton Hall and Hetton Law was fertile and laid over mostly to arable but with some livestock.

Wrangham was situated further into the Cheviots foothills where the land was good only for grazing. Here beef cattle and sheep munched on the moorland grasses.

Holborn Grange was dedicated to chicken farming and egg production where huge batteries lined the farmyard. They housed thousands of chickens in cages barely big enough for the birds to turn around in. The smell emanating from these chicken sheds was foul.

North Hazelrigg was laid over to dairy and it was to here we were sent to fetch the milk. At first my older siblings were tasked with the job but when they left for senior school or to go to work, John and I were then old enough to take on the responsibility. Most days we did this on our way home from school. We each carried a small, two-pint, white enamel milk can with fitted lids. Black splodges from the underlying steel studded the edges where the enamel had chipped. We filled the cans from the large churns stored at the dairy, or, if we were lucky and the workers had the time, the churns were left at the road end. This meant we didn't have to walk the extra quarter of a mile to and from the dairy. Sometimes, if the cows had been milked late, the milk was warm. The thick creamy liquid frothed at the rim of our cans. Our challenge was to see how far we could run without spills seeping from the lids. If we returned home with half empty cans we were sent straight back out to fill them up again. Not long afterwards the Fiddeses acquired a cow, which produced enough milk to satisfy theirs and our needs.

Hetton Steads, a small village, was the administrative headquarters for the estate. Here the wages were calculated and put into brown envelopes and distributed every Friday. Dad routinely counted his money to make sure he was given the full £2/2s/6d, barely enough to feed and clothe a family of six. He handed a quantity to Mum for housekeeping and made sure he had plenty enough for his Saturday night beer.

On occasions dances for the estate community were held in the village hall in Hetton Steads. This might be to celebrate the end of harvest, or a Christmas party. It was the only time my mother had an opportunity to dress up - not that she had much to dress up in. The same old frock each time, and it still fitted her slim figure. So restricted were her environs, the dances were a rare chance to meet and socialise with women from the other farms. Dad was luckier - every Saturday night he hopped onto the tractor and drove to the Black Bull or the White Swan in Lowick and enjoyed a pint or two (or many more) with his mates. In subsequent years a motorbike replaced the tractor. The village hall evenings gave the farm workers and their wives an opportunity to let go, relax and dance the night away to

Jimmy Shand's band tunes. Waltzes, polkas and eight-some reels, they danced them all, and what a dazzling couple my parents made as Dad swept Mum around the dance floor.

Hetton Hall was one of the larger farms in the estate, about two and a half thousand acres, and required a sizeable workforce. Dad was one of a number of permanent farm labourers who lived in the farm cottages, and was paid a standard weekly wage, plus overtime. Other itinerant workers, who came during the busy periods such as harvest time, worked on a piecework basis. Some of these men lodged in the bothy situated beside the stackyard. Three or four dirty individuals bunked in that sparse building. Other, local men would come from the surrounding villages such as Chatton and Lowick. At the end of the busy period, when the bothy men left, we broke into the building. We had no purpose in doing so but did it for the sheer boldness and thrill at the risk of getting caught. Once inside we had to hold our noses against the stench. Layers of dust coated the surfaces, filth spread across the floor, thick grease smeared the calor-gas cooker, and the mattresses' striped ticking was stained with food spills and urine. If we had any notion at all that one of the itinerants might have left behind something of worth, we were deluded.

The squalid rooms would be cleaned before the next busy period. Pity the unfortunate person who was given that job.

A concrete strip about two metres wide stretched the length of our cottages. We called it the 'Cement'. Everyday it buzzed with some activity or other. We used it for play, the weekly delivery vans parked there and opened their back doors to display their goods, and on washdays the women dragged out a mangle and wound through wet clothes and sheets. I liked to help turn the handle and watch the water drip in puddles. Across from the cottages on the other side of the Cement stood individual pigsties, one for each cottage. Usually these stored wood or tools but sometimes we had money enough to buy a piglet, which was raised for its meat. How we longed to taste the succulent pork. We fed slops to the pig, urging it to grow. Sadly the delicious meat was never bound for our dinner plates. Instead it was destined for the market to be sold for much needed cash.

Hetton Hall had a large square farmyard flanked on two sides by stone storage sheds and cattle hemmels. A granary spanned the furthest end. Here, sacks of grain were stored to dry during harvest before the grain was taken away for processing. A stone archway built beneath the granary gave entrance to more cattle hemmels behind. The hemmels were spacious sheds used to house the cattle during the cold winter months, where, by the time the beasts were packed in, they had little space in which to move. The hemmel floor was covered in straw for bedding. Hayricks stretched from one end of the building to the other on either side. These were filled with hay and served as cattle feed. Packed as they were, the animals generated so much heat that on ice-cold days steam rose from their backs. At times the smell of dung hung heavy until fresh bedding straw was laid.

Paddy, Hubert and Kath dared each other to climb the wooden beams and jump onto the backs of the cows. They were under strict instructions not to, because it caused distress to the animals, but a dare was a dare. Dad caught them once and was so incensed he beat each one in turn with the buckle end of his belt.

I often sat on the entrance gate and stroked the brows of the cows or let them lick my hand with slimy streaks of saliva. They blinked their two-inch long eyelashes at me as if to say 'open the gate and let us go free.' I worried that their lashes were too long, that they might become matted with sleep or clumped with dust.

The farm teemed with children. We regarded the farmyard and surrounding fields as a giant playground. When we had finished our chores, such as fetching kindling, chopping sticks, washing the dishes or fetching potatoes and turnips from the shed at the bottom of the slope, we disappeared out of sight of the adults to pick up whatever game we had been playing beforehand. Sometimes I preferred to play by myself and would take a ball into the farmyard and play 'donkey' against the stone wall, testing myself by throwing the ball higher and higher each time. Or I practiced hula-hoop over and over, challenging myself to beat my latest record.

By now we had been living in Hetton Hall for a few years but this account must return to 1952 to an unfinished tale. Mum pined for her distant son and when Jessie Fiddes became pregnant with Little John it reinforced Mum's need to be reunited with Joe. The time had come for my family to return to Ireland to bring him home.

# Chapter 6

# Joe's Return

How do you tell a seven-year-old boy who has lived with you as a son he will leave you soon? That he will meet his real mammy and daddy and brothers and sisters for the first time in five years. How do you tell him these strangers will take him away from Killourt, his home, to live across the sea in England? That he will go to a new school and make lots of new friends. You will always love him but his real mammy and daddy will love him just as much.

Auntie Rosie knew this conversation with Joe would be difficult and painful but was one she could put off no longer. She loved this little boy as her own. She cooked him soda bread when he was hungry, hugged him when he had a bad dream and taught him to be a good, God-fearing boy.

Joe had been two years old that cold winter at Londonderry port when, against all her motherly instincts, Mum had handed him over to her brother Mickey, who took him back to live with Rosie. Joe had no memory of his natural mother and father. Rosie was his mammy.

In Hetton Hall, our house buzzed with anticipation. We were going to Malin Head, my first holiday. It would be another five years before my family could afford to holiday again. I was two years old and would meet my grandparents, aunties, uncles and cousins for the first time.

Mum yearned to return to her beloved home, to see her family, but especially to be reunited with her third son. At the end of the holiday she would bring him to England with the rest of his family where he belonged.

My brothers and sister, inspired by the idea of a real holiday, clamoured around Mum every day and bombarded her with questions. "How many days now before we go Mam? Where will we sleep Mam? What's the boat like Mam?"

"We'll go when the time comes. Now, out of my road and leave me in peace."

Like her children Mum could hardly wait. But she knew that the job of singling the turnips had to be completed before there would be enough money for the journey.

Acres and acres of turnips waited to be thinned. Singling the crops, and picking potatoes in spring and autumn, was the only means the family had to earn extra cash over and above Dad's weekly wage. The work was paid on a piecework basis; a shilling a row, more rows, more shillings. All able-bodied family members were drafted into the fields.

Every spare daylight hour throughout the summer weeks, families lined up at the sides of large fields of seedlings. Everyone held a hoe and moved up and down the drills, row after row. They stood in the furrows between the drills to avoid damaging the tender turnip shoots. 'Swish, swish'; their hoes pushed through the earth, shifting weeds, stones and surplus seedlings into the furrows. The secret to a healthy harvest was to leave a single seedling a hoe's width from its neighbour thus enabling it to grow and expand to full size and ripeness over the season. The work was backbreaking and, from time to time, each of my family would stand upright and place their hands against the small of their back to ease the strain. While they toiled John and I either played at one end of the field or were left in the charge of neighbours. By the time we were seven we too would be bent over hoes. I remember it well, an unsentimental memory of backache and painful ribs, and the unending monotony.

Dad was the fastest. Up and down the rows he raced, like a whippet; frenetic, determined. 'Swish, swish, swish, swish.'

"Get a move on. Put your backs into it," he would shout.

"Hmphh. It's all right for him," Paddy and Hubert would grumble, "He's bigga an stronga than us."

Mum would raise her eyebrows in quiet disapproval. "We could all single as fast as him if we left half the weeds and turnips in the rows like he does."

"Stop your blethering woman. Do yer think the boss is gonna walk up and down every row inspecting? Is he buggery. He won't step foot in the field when we leave it. If they paid a few extra shillings I might be bothered, but they don't, so I'm not."

You had to hand it to Dad, he was a grafter and if he hadn't been as fast we would have had less money for the holiday. He needed the break as much as anyone, probably more so, and he wanted enough spare cash to enjoy himself while we were away. After all, in England he never had the chance to drink real Irish Guinness with his pals.

After weeks of laborious, dreary work my family had accumulated enough cash for just one week's holiday.

So it was that in August 1952 we boarded the cattle boat at Glasgow port and braced ourselves for the long, gruelling trip to Ireland.

The bus from Londonderry port dropped us at the Malin Head crossroads. The pungent smell of burning peat lingered in the air. More than anything it is this smell I would come to identify with the area; the incense of Malin Head.

Dad pointed to the west where, across the bay in the distance, the land rose in a series of peaks. He said, "Them's the Sperrin Mountains. The biggest you can see there, well, that's Slieve Snaght, the highest in Inishowen. Plenty's a time I've been up that mountain to cut peat from the bog. Bloody hard work I can tell you. Harder than singling mind. We had to haul the load back down the mountain in all weathers and stack it in the turf sheds to dry."

"We wouldn't have had warm fires in winter without it," Mum said. "Sometimes we hung fish from the mantelpiece to smoke. The peat gave it a special flavour. You never tasted the like, delicious."

She went on to describe how they gathered dulce seaweed from the shore, dried it and ate it. "Full of the goodness," she said.

I tasted it once and never again. The flavour made me think of chewy salted shoe leather.

"We collected carrigon moss off the rocks and dried that too," she said. "It turned pure white. Mammy boiled it with milk and sugar to make a pudding. People also made it into a drink to help their bad chests."

As my parents reminisced we walked the mile from the crossroads along the shore road to Killourt, where my mother had grown up. When the tides were high and the ocean ferocious, shingle from the beach was whipped up and thrown across the road, making it impassable. But this day the Atlantic lay still and quiet. The outgoing tide exposed large expanses of dark rock and rock pools teeming with life. Oystercatcher pipings pierced the salt air and eider ducks paddled the gentle waves. Thatched cottages dotted the hillsides. Their tiny window frames and stable doors painted a bright red or green, contrasted with the whitewashed stone. Wisps of peat smoke rose from the chimneys and added to the already laden air.

"I'm home," Mum said as she breathed in large gulps of Killourt. Her heart had remained here. She always said her stay in England was temporary and she would return one day, never to leave again. Dad, much less rooted, saw the north east of England as a place of greater opportunity.

Rosie lingered by the cottage gate waiting for us, her red hair tied in a bun at the nape of her neck. Granda stood tall in the doorway, smiling. Mum clearly inherited her dark hair and height from her father. The absence of Granny by his side must have been a great source of anguish to Mum. How could she have known, when she waved goodbye to her mother that day five years ago, she would never see her again. Many times Mum told me her mother had been an angel on earth; nobody had been as good and beautiful as her. She said Granny's long blonde hair was as soft as pillow feathers. During the day she wrapped it out of sight in a bun but at night it fell down her back in waves, like an angel. Now she was an angel in heaven.

On either side of Rosie stood Joe and her own daughter Anne, now a three year old. Rosie had married two years after Mum left Malin Head and was pregnant again with her second child. Joe watched us approach. Small for his age and skinny, he resembled Hubert, except his hair was not as dark. If ever there had been any doubt, the distinctive Toland nostril flare singled him out as a true sibling.

Mum bent down to Joe's level and smiled. Here at last, her son.

"Hello Joe," she said as she touched his face and hair. "What a handsome fella you are."

The feel and warmth of his skin made her glow with love. Desperate to hold him close she put her arms around his thin waist to pick him up but he pushed her back, and stood closer still to Rosie.

"Give him time Sadie," Rosie said. "He'll come round."

A week of re-acquaintance began. Paddy and Hubert were old enough to remember Joe, Kathleen less so, but to John and me, he was a stranger.

Mum took us aside and said, "This is your brother."

Paddy, Hubert and Kathleen enjoyed a week of freedom from the fields of Hetton Hall and spent the entire time at play with our cousins. John and I were too young yet to join them. They clambered the crags high above the shoreline and splashed about in the rock pools. To them, one week felt like an entire summer. For the women, one week was pitifully fleeting. How could you get to know a child and that child gain your trust in such a short time? How could you get used to the idea of giving up a child after five years of care? Mum and Rosie both struggled in their own way. As sisters, they were close and during that one-week they enjoyed each other's company; they sat in front of the fire, drank tea and smoked cigarettes. Nicotine stains smeared each woman's fingers and cigarette smoke hovered in a fug above their reminiscences. They chatted about old times and laughed at the tricks their younger selves had gotten up to. But beneath the laughter each woman sensed the other's torment.

Dad on the other hand enjoyed his Guinness. The local pubs in Malin Head were licenced to stay open until two or three in the morning to cater for the fishermen who fished all day and night. The boats would motor in to the harbour at around midnight, the fishermen dying of thirst – a thirst that water would not quench. Dad met his pals at Farrens Bar or Docs and revelled until the early hours. When their drinking was done they could hardly stand upright, let alone stumble home in the 'wee' hours. The amount of money Dad spent on his Guinness, it is no wonder he forced us to work the fields singling and potato picking for weeks and weeks.

On the day of departure the Killourt community spilled out of their cottages and gathered to say farewell. Joe had been part of their lives; the least they could do was say goodbye to the little man. My brothers and sister stood among their cousins downcast, sad to be leaving.

Granda picked up Joe and hugged him hard and said, "You be a good boy now for Mammy and Daddy." Granda had grown to love Joe dearly. To think this wee boy would no longer be running about the place and getting under his feet, he struggled to hold back the tears.

Mum held Joe's hand determined her son would not be left behind this time. Rosie knew she had no claim to him, yet when the moment came to say goodbye she could no longer contain her buried emotions. She became distraught and sobbed uncontrollably. An onlooker might have thought someone had died. Perhaps that is how Rosie felt that day.

Confused and bewildered by Rosie's wails Joe began to cry, "I want to stay with Rosie."

He pulled his had away from Mum's and made to move toward Rosie but Dad gathered him in his grasp. Joe squirmed and stretched forward to clutch at Rosie's clothes desperate to hang on to this woman who made him feel safe.

"No, no. I want to stay with Rosie."

Mum clasped her hands against her chest as if to shield the blow of Joe's cries. Her emotions were a turmoil of guilt, heartbreak and resolve. Guilt, that she was causing such sorrow to her father and sister; heartbreak for a son who refused to accept her; resolve, that she would give him a better future and that, in time, he would grow to love her as his real mammy.

Normally Dad had little time for emotional outbursts but the wretched scene that confronted him softened even his hard core. Rosie's grief, Granda's torment and Joe's hysteria prompted him to propose a compromise.

"Rosie, we can leave Hubert here for a time. You can take care of him instead. I will come and fetch him when I can."

Hubert's eyes lit up and his mouth spread into the biggest smile. He loved Killourt and, for a while at least, he would be spared the rod. Paddy looked sullen and clearly wished he had been chosen. Mum protested; she wanted all her family by her side, looked after by her, not by a surrogate parent, even if that surrogate was her beloved sister. But when Dad made up his mind she had little say in the matter. Hubert was older, eleven years old, and plainly delighted. Perhaps this decision was easier for her to bear than the one of five years ago.

Joe ceased his crying when Dad took out his watch from his pocket and dangled it in front of him. Dad told Joe he could keep it if he came away with us. This shiny, ticking timepiece was a powerful persuader.

When we stepped aboard the return cattle boat, once again we were an incomplete family.

Joe struggled with his new life in Hetton Hall. He wasn't even allowed to keep the watch. He withdrew into himself and cried a lot. If home life was difficult, school was torture. The schoolchildren bullied him for his strange accent; for his puny size and for his apparent inability to learn. The headmaster wrote in his school report, *'If Joe ever had any brains he lost them a long time ago.'*

If bullying wasn't enough at school, reports like this prompted bullying at home too, from Dad and Paddy. Dad found it difficult to accept that a son of his could be so stupid, and Paddy, who had a reputation to maintain among his pals, was ashamed to be his brother. As it turned out, Joe was far from stupid; he just didn't care for academic subjects; or perhaps it was his unhappiness that blocked his learning.

Mum protected him as much as she could but as far as Joe was concerned she was a stranger to him. This small once happy, carefree boy, yanked from a warm and secure home in Malin Head, began to 'wet the bed'. His humiliation was complete.

Over time the bullying at home lessened and Joe began to accept us as his family. He no longer yearned for Rosie but he had a separateness that stayed with him throughout his life. Such a trauma at an impressionable age was bound to have deep-seated implications.

One day, a year later, Dad walked up the slope to the cottage with a dark-haired boy, who looked a lot like Joe. Dad had taken a quick trip to Ireland and brought Hubert home. I had no memory of this boy; a year is a long time to a two-year-old and now I had yet another brother to become acquainted with.

Hubert had returned and for the first time our family was complete.

# Chapter 7

# The Thompsons

Like most farms in the area, Hetton Hall had a 'Big House' associated with it, which would have originally belonged to the landowner or squire – before being bought by the CWS.

The 'Big House', a baronial gothic style, grey stone, three storey construction stood a few metres from the farm buildings, set within its own six acres of land. I thought, '*it must be a castle.*'

It was first built as a 'Tower House' in the 15th century as a defence against marauding Scots. Originally it had a turreted roof, which was later replaced by slate. At one time the tower had been recommended as a garrison for about twenty men. It is not known if this ever happened. A stone spiral staircase led from the second floor to the top floor. In the 18th and 19th centuries new wings were built to the east, west and rear. Unattractive and menacing, in present day it is a Grade II listed building.

The Thompson family occupied the Big House. They rented it from the CWS. We called it the Thompsons' House. Mr and Mrs Thompson were well spoken. They owned five ponies that grazed in their fields and they sent their three daughters and son to boarding school when they reached secondary school age. We, with our broad Northumbrian accents, thought them rich and posh.

Through the friendship with the two youngest siblings, Hilary and Mark, we Toland children were allowed over the threshold of the *castle*. The other farm children never gained this privilege. The two older daughters, Althea and Judith were away from home much of the time, either at boarding school or subsequently at work, so we had little to do with them.

During the school holidays, when Hilary was home from boarding school, she and my sister Kathleen were the best of friends. To our delight she often invited us to ride the ponies. Mokka was my favourite. His four white fetlocks matched the white slash that stretched from his forehead to his nose. His mane and forelock were the colour of straw, the perfect contrast to his honey brown body. I thought him the most handsome animal in the entire world. In the summer months I would sit on the gate by the meadow and call to him. He would lift his head from his grazing and trot over to me. I talked to him at length while he nudged his velvet muzzle into my hands. I fancied he and I had a special bond, and woe betide anyone who told me horses were stupid. Mokka's intelligence was unquestionable and he understood every word I said.

We helped Hilary lead the ponies from the meadow to the stables in the yard of the house. She showed us how to brush and saddle them. She taught us the name of each tack item, which hung in neat rows in the tack room. When the time came for me to sit astride a pony for the first time my nerves tingled. I was six years old. I stood on a stool and hauled myself across the saddle, belly first. The pony shifted its weight from one hoof to another just as I tried to straddle him causing me to wobble and fall to the ground.

After a couple more attempts I sat tall and proud and tried to ignore the vast distance between the stable yard floor and myself. Hilary helped me put my feet in the stirrups, set high to allow my little legs to reach, and she showed me the proper way to hold the reins. The musky pony smell, the squeak of leather and the touch of reins in my hands, made me feel grand and brave. As soon as Hilary released the bridle and let me take charge, the pony began to move unbidden and I had no control whatsoever. My bravery soon turned to fear.

Before long I too was trotting a pony around the paddock shouting to John, 'Look at me, look at me.' I sorely wanted to canter and gallop like real riders but didn't have the courage to do so. Not yet. I envied John his natural ability. He cantered, galloped and even jumped the 'jumps'.[6]

One day, while John was showing off his riding skills, my pony became excited and broke into a gallop. This took me completely by surprise. A trot was the fastest I had ridden up to that point. The grass rushed past below me at an alarming speed. I fumbled with the reins and tried hard to make the pony slow down. But still we galloped on. As panic took hold it was all I could do to stay in the saddle. Pounding hooves echoed in my head blocking out all other sound. I lost grip of the reins and struggled to grasp a handful of the pony's mane. When it headed straight towards the barb-wired fence at the edge of the field I felt sure my life would end that day. We would both be ripped to shreds. Sensing danger moments before

---

6 Years later he would jump much taller 'jumps' as a jockey in steeplechase races, wearing the colours of Arthur Stevenson.

impact the pony came to an abrupt halt. I flew over its head to land inches away from the spiky barbs. Some time would pass before I found the courage to climb on a pony again.

Joe also liked to ride the ponies and he would go on cross-country tacks with Hilary. He was a competent rider but had a reckless streak, which often found him in trouble. One day he and Hilary were trekking over the fields. They approached a sizeable ditch and while anyone with any sense would have found a way around it, Joe was sweet on Hilary and wished to impress her. He kicked the pony into a canter and made to jump the trench. The pony stumbled, Joe tumbled, and the poor animal fell heavily on top of Joe's foot causing a bone to crack. He could not walk. Somehow Hilary helped him back on the pony and they made their way home. What a drama it created. Jessie Fiddes rushed to phone the ambulance, Mum fussed over Joe, and John and I were shooed out of the way. When the ambulance drove up the slope to our cottage John and I tussled one another to peer inside at the fascinating equipment; a stretcher on wheels, an oxygen canister, tubes, all manner of weird implements of which we had no notion.

"Will you turn on the siren?"

"Will you make the blue light flash?"

"Will yous two move out of the way of the ambulance driver?" Mum shouted at us for bothering him.

Neighbours piled onto the Cement to see Joe being wheeled from the cottage in a wheelchair, his face creased in pain. And no wonder – a metatarsal bone protruded through his skin. The neighbours expressed, "Ooos and ahhs," in sympathy. Joe had suffered a compound fracture and was taken to hospital to have his foot encased in a plaster cast.[7]

Mark Thompson, six months my junior, was a dark haired boy whose fine features belied his mischievous nature. He wasn't yet old enough to join his sisters at boarding school and until then he attended Hazelrigg Primary School with us. John and Mark became firm buddies. The pair would be gone for hours and only came home when hunger demanded. Sometimes I was permitted to tag along but most of the time it was just the two of them. Who knows what the pair got up to, they kept their adventures to themselves. Mostly...

...One afternoon John ran into the house bursting to share his story.

---

7 A similar incident occurred many years later; a different ditch, a different broken bone in a different time. Joe had grown up and his reckless streak had grown with him. In 1966, on the day before Kathleen's wedding in southern England, Joe invited Nina, one of Kathleen's best friends, to go out for a ride with him on his motorbike. Nina, a Geordie lass, had travelled south for the wedding.
"Wey aye man, let's do it," she said.
Off they sped on the motorbike. They didn't hear Kathleen's words trailing after them, "You make sure you look after her, our Joe."
I'm sure he had every intention of doing so but I wonder if he was sweet on Nina too and wanted to impress. His bravado got the better of him. He took a corner too fast and they skidded into a ditch. They made a sorry but comical pair in church the next day and almost stole the show from the bride. All eyes peered at them as they made their entrance. Nina, dressed in her posh frock festooned with pink flowers, Joe in his smart grey suit, they both struggled down the aisle on crutches with their left legs in plaster cast. They banged against and knocked the woodwork as they manoeuvred into end pews. When everyone stood to welcome the bride Joe and Nina sat with their broken legs stuck out into the aisle smiling the sheepish smile of guilty children.

"Mam. Mam, you never guess what Mark and I just saw?"

"What did you see?" Mum asked.

"We saw this egg coming oot o' the hole in the ground by the hen hoose. It was doin' it all by itself. We thought it was magic. And then we saw the rat's whiskers and then the rat. It was pushin' the egg oot. And then another rat came oot o' the hole as well. And then the two rats started pushin' the egg o'er the ground. And then ... "

He couldn't get the words out fast enough. Mum urged him to slow down. He went on to explain how both rats gently nudged the egg over the grass until they reached a rough gravel patch. One rat turned onto its back and the second picked up the egg in its paws and laid it onto the first one's belly. John said the rat on its back held onto the egg while the other grabbed it by its tail and dragged it over the gravel.

"...and then when they got back to the grassy bit the rat on its back turned over and they both started pushin' the egg again."

Mum listened to John's story and immediately clipped his ear. She said, "Don't tell fibs John Toland. It's a sin do yer hear me. You'll go to hell, do yer know that."

"But it's true! We did see it."

Mum clipped his ear again and told him to take himself and his lies out of her sight. Poor John, he rubbed his smarting ear and stomped off fuming at the world's injustices.

Mum didn't believe him but John swears by the memory. It is quite feasible rats might steal an egg to take to their nest to feed to their young. They are clever creatures and find ways to overcome difficulties such as how to prevent a raw egg from being smashed on rough ground.

One day John and I were playing in the farmyard waiting for Mark to join us. We saw him walk around the corner from his house inching his way along with his arms outstretched.

"Eee, whats he doin' now?' asked John. As If I should know.

Mark's eyes were tight shut. He fooled around a lot and we thought nothing of his behaviour. To humour him we ran up and said, "What yer doin' Mark? What yer doin' with your eyes closed?"

Then we noticed his eyes were not just closed but swollen. So swollen he could not open them. To demonstrate he lifted his head upwards and with all his might tried to prise his eyes apart but they remained firmly shut.

"What's happened to yer eyes?" John asked.

"I got stung by a massive bumblebee. You should have seen it." Mark held his thumb and forefinger apart by an exaggerated distance to indicate the size of the bee.

He struggled to point to the bridge of his nose where the bee had landed. "I smacked at it to get it off, and then it stung me."

Mark suffered a severe reaction to the bee sting and for several days he wandered about the farmyard blind. John and I took every opportunity to trick him.

"This way Mark. The path's o'er here."

He followed our voices as we led him into a wall or a hedge. How we laughed when he bumped against the stone, or stumbled against bushes. We weren't so cruel as to lead him into nettle patches but we were tempted. He soon stopped trusting our instructions and, using a sturdy staff, found his own way. His mother tried to keep him indoors until the swelling reduced but he would have none of it. Nothing was going to stop him going out to play, not even blindness. After three days he could open his eyes halfway. Three more days and his sight returned to normal.

We rarely saw Mr Thompson but when we did he was kind to us. He spent most of his day out on his land fixing fences, tending his crops, or seeing to the ponies. He had had a distinguished Second World War career and was awarded the DSO for his services as a bomber pilot. Mrs Thompson, a tall commanding woman, with dark hair pulled back in a bun, was a little scary but she tolerated us as we ran through the house. We would bound up the wooden back stairs, which led from the kitchen to the second floor, dart along the corridor the full length of the house, then down the carpeted front stairs, two at a time, and out of the front door. We would run around to the back of the house to do it all over again. Mark led the way and John and I followed. Sometimes the sitting room door was open and I would peek a glance at the smart, floral covered couches and think how soft and comfortable they looked compared to our scrabby leather sofa. Mrs Thompson must have been irritated with the noise and clatter of our footsteps and high-pitched yells but perhaps she was glad Mark had playmates his own age among a houseful of older sisters. We were forbidden from venturing up the mysterious, dark spiral staircase to the third floor. For a long time I imagined ghoulish creatures lurked beyond but it turned out, to my disappointment, that nothing nasty hid in the rooms above. The stairs were dangerous and needed repair, and therefore off-limits.

When Mark first invited us into his kitchen John and I stood open-mouthed at the size of the space. Our entire cottage could have fitted into this one room. And to think the house contained many rooms just as big, and all those staircases. It confirmed my belief this *was a castle*.

The lawn to the front of the house sloped gradually toward the fields. In summer the family sometimes held garden parties. Mum told us to keep well away when these took place. We ignored her and crept into the field where we could get a good view of the posh people without being seen. Men and women mingled on the lawn dressed in expensive clothes and drank wine and ate 'titbits'. Althea held her wedding reception on the lawn. This was a grand affair; top hats and tails, elegant dresses and popping champagne bottles. Hetton Hall had never witnessed such a spectacle.

At Easter-time we rolled decorated hard-boiled eggs down the lawn slope and held competitions to see whose egg would crack first. Egg decoration was a serious business. First we gathered items that would create intricate patterns on the shell; ferns, primroses, onionskins. Then we dampened our eggs and stuck on the leafage in our own haphazard way. We wrapped each in a piece of old non-colourfast cloth and Mum lowered our parcels into a pan of boiling water. She cooked the eggs until the water turned the colour of the cloth. We waited, impatient to untie it and peel back the foliage to reveal what we had created. The dye from the cloth stained the parts of the egg that were not covered with leafage, leaving a perfect white imprint of the fern or primrose.

We had a similar competition at Hazelrigg School. Every pupil brought in a decorated egg and Mr Wright, the headmaster, placed it in a large round container with a flat mesh bottom, like a sieve. Twenty pairs of eyes watched him as he lightly tipped the container from side to side. The brightly coloured orbs rolled and rocked against one another until, after a few seconds, he stopped tipping. He then picked up each egg in turn and examined it for cracks. The disappointed owners saw their cracked eggs removed from the container and out of the competition. Mr Wright repeated this process until only one uncracked egg remained and declared the winner. My egg never won.

A small copse stood adjacent to the Thompsons' lawn behind a stone wall. Many an hour John, Mark and I played hide and seek amongst the trees or climbed the branches, our voices echoing through the leaves.

"Higher. Dare you."

I didn't have the courage to climb as high as the two boys. I preferred to remain in the lower branches and ignored their jeers. Thousands of spring daffodils interspersed with purple crocuses, like dabs of ink on a soft yellow blanket, studded the wood. I stared at them full of wonder that so many, many flowers bloomed in one place. Mrs Thompson let me pick bunches for my mother.

The hot summer days seemed to last forever. I barely remember any rain. When we weren't singling, chopping wood or collecting kindling for the fire we were out all day. As long as we didn't get in the adults' way, we had freedom to roam and the Thompson children roamed with us. They exposed us to activities we would never have had the opportunity to do otherwise and without a doubt they enriched and enlarged our young lives.

# Chapter 8

# The Collinses

Soon after we moved into the top cottage, when I was three, the Collins family moved into the middle cottage - Big James, Rose and their three children, Rosemary, Evelyn and Little James. Like us they were Irish immigrants from Donegal seeking a better life.

Big James, a six foot dark haired man with gentle smiling eyes that twinkled with mischief, came from Clonmany, a small town about twelve miles southwest of Malin Head. My parents and he had been unacquainted in Ireland. In such a remote and rural area as was north Donegal, twelve miles was a long way. Big James always wore bibbed blue overalls cinched at his waist with a black leather belt. When the belt became worn he replaced it with a piece of binder-twine. He rescued me the night of my 'man in the moon' visitation; only he heard my yells. On another occasion he rescued Joe from strangling himself with a piece of rubber hose. Joe had wound the tubing around his neck several times and could not unwind it. He had turned blue by the time Big James found him.

He also rescued himself - this time from Joe. Some months after the rubber hose incident Joe picked up a loaded shotgun that had been carelessly left against the farmyard wall - the perfect weapon for a cowboy. Big

James sauntered into the yard and Joe spotted his victim. He pointed his rifle at the older man's chest.

"Hands up or I'll shoot," he said as his eight-year-old fingers curled around the trigger.

Startled and alarmed Big James said, "Give me the gun Joe, there's a good lad," his voice barely a whisper.

He knew Joe would have no idea he held a loaded gun but James also knew Joe understood how to pull the trigger. He took a step closer.

"Come on son. Give me the gun, now."

"No. I found it. I want to play with it."

Joe waved the gun up and down. Big James knew if he didn't take the gun from the boy soon he might lose his life. He took a deep breath and stepped closer still.

"Joe, GIVE ME THE GUN!"

Perhaps the urgency and tremor in James' voice, or the fearful look on his pallid face, prompted Joe to lower the gun and hand it over. Or maybe the fear of the strap from Dad helped persuade him.

He was spared the strap but received a strong lecture about playing with loaded shotguns.

Big James was an uneducated man. As he settled in to the work on the farm he became the target of unkind jokes and jibes from the other workers, including my dad.

What James lacked in learning and sophistication he made up for with hard work, which the men could not deny.

His wife Rose, on the other hand, had more than her share of intellect. She cleverly manipulated her husband to 'get her own way'. By her own admission if she thought he would say "No," she beguiled him into thinking it was his idea, and generally got what she wanted.

Her build was slight and she had red hair and freckles. Her square jaw and straight nose made for sharp features. A storyteller and a poet, she had many funny tales to tell. She told a story and retold it several times in one sitting, just in case you missed the point of the joke the first time around, or the second, or even the third. This rather spoiled the impact of what, in the original telling, was an interesting and amusing tale.

Rose hailed from a place called Dreena, situated among the bleak moors about five miles inland from Malin Head. She shared her maiden name, McLaughlin, with Mum but they were unrelated. Rose's family had been large and poverty-stricken and although Mum had never met the family she had heard rumours about their hardship. "Their clothes were ragged and dirty. Sometimes they went wi' out shoes and they often went hungry," she said. My parents also lived on the edge but they always had enough to eat and shoes to wear.

The intellectual differences between Big James and Rose made them an unlikely couple, but he was devoted to her. She almost certainly married him to escape impoverishment. Perhaps the lack of sustenance as a child led Rose to become a sickly woman, or at times feign sickness, as my parents suspected. She had charm and intrigue and would do anything for my family. She and Mum became good friends, a friendship that lasted sixty years. I liked her too - a lot. In my pre-school years she gave me biscuits. One day I wandered into her cottage and asked if I could have one.

She said, "Oh, I'm sorry little one but your mammy said I wasn't to give you any more biscuits."

"That's alright," I replied. "I'll just take one," and I walked to the sideboard cupboard without a 'please' or a 'thank you', and helped myself. This was one of the stories Rose told and retold.

Their eldest daughter, Rosemary, inherited her mother's red hair and freckles, and her ability to be repeatedly anecdotal. She was three years older than me. Her younger sister Evelyn, in contrast, was a dark-haired beauty, who, like her father, had smiling eyes. She was two years older than me to the day and shared a birthday on October 13th. We became firm buddies, another friendship that lasted well into adulthood.

I held these two girls in the highest regard and wanted to be just like them. They were on a pedestal I longed to climb. I followed them around the farm and felt privileged when they let me join in their games. We formed a 'secret society', which strictly forbade boys. An abandoned pigsty behind the stack yard served as our headquarters. We laboured to clear the pigsty and threw out rubbish, swept the floor clean and dragged in straw bales for seats.

Fuelled by comic books and imagination we called ourselves the "Hetton Hall Girls Secret Society." But to be secret we needed to conceal our identities. We each fashioned ourselves a garment, like a nun's habit, from empty potato sacks. We cut a slit to pull over our heads and two holes for our arms, and tied the garment around the waist with binder twine. We also made hoods to hide our faces, like the Ku Klux Klan. Inside our headquarters we devised a secret code only we three could decipher. We thought it devilishly clever. Our aim was to document a plan about how to save the world.

'Ew Era Gniog ot Evas eht Dlrow' - *We Are Going to Save the World*

1. Slrig lliw eb eht sessob - *Girls will be the bosses*
2. Syob lliw eb eht sevals - *Boys will be the slaves*
3. ...

The list continued. The boys tried but failed to break the code - words written backwards - and charged off infuriated, muttering about 'stupid girl games'.

The "Hetton Hall Girls Secret Society" lasted a few weeks until we tired of the itchy musty uniform and could no longer think of ways to save the planet.

Little James, also a redhead, had his father's features, which included those smiling eyes. He too had a story-telling flair. He was two years my junior and as cute as they come. I told him many times I would marry him when we were older.

Soon after the family arrived in Hetton Hall Rose became pregnant and gave birth to her fourth child, Anthony, a roly-poly and completely bald baby. He wore a woolly blue romper suit, which had a hood with pointed ears, like a cat. He wore this until his arms and legs reached inches below the cuffs and his chubby head burst through the seams. As Anthony grew more mobile he became an impish rascal, with no sense at all. He spent his small life searching for the next obstacle to climb. His mother despaired trying to keep an eye on him. She turned from her chores one day to discover he had disappeared from the house. She couldn't believe what she saw when she found him. He had wandered out of the front door, climbed a stone wall and reached for the washing line tied to a post that butted up to the wall. The eighteen-month-old boy hung suspended from the line by his armpits. His little legs dangled in mid-air unable to move forward or backward. How he remained suspended without tumbling is a mystery.

"Sheer instinct and will," said Rose. She whisked her youngest to safety and afterwards laughed at his intrepid nature. She immediately added the episode to her bag of stories, to be told time and again.

When Anthony's hair finally grew the maternal red gene prevailed and so too did the paternal smiling eyes.

When my family moved from the top cottage the Collinses moved in. It was like playing musical houses. Each new family would begin life in Hetton Hall in the middle cottage and when the music stopped would grab the next biggest cottage (the top). When the music stopped again it would be into the largest (the bottom), which is where we moved.

A year or two later, damp began to seep through our living room floor. The same was true of the other cottages and, as winter approached, would only get worse if left unattended. My parents worried for our health and their scant possessions, as did the other tenants. After several collective complaints the CWS agreed to upgrade the stone floors. Our cottage was the first to be upgraded. The floor was to be laid with asphalt, a black tar like substance, which was resilient and damp proof but which gave off strong fumes. Because the fumes were toxic we were told to move out while they carried out the work. Our whole family decamped and moved in with the Collinses until the fumes subsided. Five adults (this included Paddy), and nine children squeezed into two bedrooms and a small living room. I have no memory of the adults sleeping arrangements but we children moulded into two three-quarter sized beds in one room, two at the top of the bed and two at the bottom; girls in one and boys in the other. Anthony slept in a cot in his parent's room. We had fun at the start but after several blunt prods in the face from careless feet and bedclothes being yanked away, the fun rapidly deteriorated into whines and grumbles.

"Will yer stop kicking me in the face?"

"Well will you stop pulling off the blankets?"

We lived with the Collinses approximately a week. Living in such close proximity must have been difficult and tense for the adults. Fourteen people shared one toilet and one bathroom. Even my mother's capacity for tolerance was tested that week. I was forced to become used to weak tea and bread with margarine – we always had butter in our own house.

My dad said, "Where's the bloody tea? It's boiled water and milk!" He had a point. By the week's end the *margarine* didn't taste too bad at all. It shows you can get used to anything if you have no choice. Although when we moved back home my first request was for a slice of bread with butter.

A week later we did it all over again, except the other way around. At least in our house the Collinses were served a decent cup of tea.

Rose's brother, John McLaughlin, came to stay one summer season to work and help with the harvest. Rose made a bed for him on their couch and he squeezed into their family life as if he had always been a part.

John was a wiry man, a heavy drinker and a bad influence on my father. He encouraged Dad to drink more than was good for him. The pair regularly headed to the Lowick pubs on Dad's motorbike. After closing time the two drunken men would sit astride the bike and wrestle with the machine to keep it upright on the dark, deserted country roads; this, while all the time singing loudly into the night, terrorising the wildlife in the hedgerows. They would stumble into the house and slur and stagger around the living room, like rowdy students. My mother would grumble to herself but made them tea all the same.

Big James abstained from these drunken sprees. His father had been an alcoholic, which had brought his family much anxiety and shame. James vowed to avoid his father's example and at the age of eighteen he took 'The Pledge'. He remained true to his abstinence all his life and never knowingly drank alcohol, even on special occasions such as his daughters' weddings.

John McLaughlin barely pulled his weight on the farm but he had a sharp wit and kept the other labourers amused for which they mostly forgave him his idleness. He teased and flirted with Mum and would pick her up and carry her about and drop her on a chair or some other safe place.

Mum, who enjoyed this attention would say, "He's full of the divilment that man. What will he do next?"

What he did next was release the Fiddeses fat pink sow from the pigsty and ride it bareback up and down the Cement, like an Indian brave. He encouraged the other adults to take turns, including my mother. She straddled the beast and when it began to trot forward she cried out, "Jesus, will yous make it stop." We children giggled helplessly while the abused pig squealed with rage, or fright. When Jessie Fiddes discovered what they were up to she too squealed with rage. "Put it back, do you here! Right this minute."

Jessie cared little for John McLaughlin and his childish antics. She stood behind him and supervised, like a stern head mistress, as he returned the sow to the pigsty. The poor animal slunk to the back and kept as far out of sight as possible.

Life in the middle of nowhere could be achingly dull. John, a man who bored easily, determined to bring some fun to the stale existence. He invented one prank after another and many an evening laughter erupted and spilled from one or other of the three cottages. Big John and Jessie Fiddes, excluded from the frivolity, could only listen from the bottom of the slope. The farm steward and his wife were uninvited.

At the season's end John left the farm and headed south to find work in the building trade. The farm workers missed his fun but not his indolence.

Other relatives of Rose came and went, some from Ireland, some from America. The American visitors were the most exciting. They had money and exotic possessions. They usually brought a selection of cast-off clothes, which Rosemary and Evelyn fought over. The girls were a year apart and a similar height therefore they scrapped over who should have what. It mattered not that the clothes were second hand, to them they were bright and shining, and worth a few hair pulls and face scratches.

One of their American visitors owned a Brownie camera. He liked to set up compositions to show off his artistic abilities. One such composition consisted of an old-fashioned brown leather armchair as the main prop. The chair had been thrown out onto the Cement ready to be dumped. A spring, tangled with horsehair stuffing, poked through the cushion. The arms and back were scuffed with wear and tear and for a few days we youngsters used it as part of an obstacle course.

The visitor ordered us to take up positions around the chair. I sat on the seat alongside Little James. Anthony, still in his blue romper suit, sat on his lap. A baby girl, who belonged to Rose's sister Susan, sat in my lap. The older children stood by the arms and back of the chair in height order. We were instructed to stay perfectly still until the visitor clicked the shutter. This may well have been the first time I had my photo taken and seen the result. What a rag-tag bunch we made.

Standing: John, Rosemary Collins, Joe, Hubert, Kathleen, Evelyn Collins
Sitting: Unknown Baby, Margaret (Me), James Collins, Anthony Collins

After six years in Hetton Hall the Collinses moved to the chicken farm at Holborn Grange, two and a half miles away. This was an opportunity for the family to earn more money and live in larger accommodation. Rose was pregnant again with their daughter Patricia so they needed the extra space. The farm consisted of two huge batteries, which housed thousands of chickens. Feeding troughs extended the length of the batteries and to reach the seed the chickens had to poke their heads out of a small gap. Rows and rows of pitiful combs, faded from lack of sunlight, bobbed in unison as the wretched birds pecked at the seed. Each day, as Rose collected the eggs, she was forced to withstand the noxious smell that emanated from the cages and the cacophony of cackles, which filled the battery. Big James had the worst job. He waded through mounds of chicken dung to shovel and bag it for fertilizer production.

From Holborn Grange a grassy track led uphill about a mile to the moors and into the woodland where St Cuthbert's Cave could be found. The locals called it 'Cuddy's Cove'. Looking back from the track was a fine view of the distant Cheviot Hills. Hidden among tall pine trees the natural cave had been carved over millennia of erosion from a large sandstone outcrop. The rocks and cave were a haven for children; perfect to clamber over and build fires within. People said it had been a rest stop for St Cuthbert's body en-route from Lindisfarne to his final resting place at Durham Cathedral.[8]

---

8 The St Cuthbert legend prevails and in present day the cave is a tourist attraction, which belongs to the National Trust.

In the summer months I walked the two and a half miles to Holborn Grange with my brothers and sister to play with Rosemary and Evelyn - eager to explore Cuddy's Cove. I wanted desperately to go up to the moors with them but when I tagged behind, my brothers always said, "There's snakes up there. Big adders hiding in the bracken." This was a ploy to frighten me to stay behind. Being younger I would only hold them back. It worked. I hated snakes. My mother tried to reassure me and said, "They are just trying to scare you. You go along with them."

Hours I would wait. When they returned they were full of tales of their adventures, which made me intensely envious. But, despite my desperation to join them, I never did overcome my snake fear. Instead I hung around the batteries and played with Little James and Anthony or helped Rose collect eggs.

In 1961 the Collins family followed Rose's brother John south to Clacton-on-Sea, Essex. He told them of the many well-paid job opportunities in the building trade there. They could earn twice the amount of chicken farm wages. The family packed their belongings and headed south.

This would not be the last we saw of them, as we would meet up again in later years.

# Chapter 9

# The Burn

The Burn meandered across the countryside like a snake, slithering its way from a spring a few miles north to join the River Till further south near Wooler. On the other side of the fence from the field we took to go to school, it formed a large pond wider and deeper than the rest of its course. An old stone road bridge spanned the Burn. In spring primroses and celandines crowded the banks. Marsh marigolds brightened the boggy areas, like little cups of gold. The Burn narrowed in places but never enough to jump across without getting wet. The only way to cross it was to wade.

We gathered there to play and wade out of sight of the adults. The Burn came alive in the summer months with our cries and squeals.

"Come on, let's paddle."

"No, let's go fishing."

June Fiddes and I could be seen barefoot at the stream's edge, our socks and sandals thrown off and scattered on the bank. Our dress hems skimmed the water's surface as we hunkered down and fished for minnows and sticklebacks. We lowered our jam jars and used the string tied around the neck to drag them through the water. Then we scooped the jars up and out and examined how many tiny fish we had caught. Often the fish eluded us but sometimes we found a rich patch and caught several. We took little interest in their beauty and were heedless of their metallic green and blue sheens and vivid red undertones. Instead, we sat on the bank and counted the sticklebacks' spines, which became magnified by the water in the jars - sometimes we counted two, sometimes four, but mostly three.

When John and I were still of pre-school age we were forbidden to play at the Burn unless accompanied by Kathleen. My mother insisted Kathleen take us, despite her pleas. Older sisters were expected to be responsible for younger siblings. Older brothers were far too important for such a duty, or at least they considered themselves to be. Like washing up or dusting furniture – those were girl's chores. Kathleen would sooner have the freedom to play with her friend Hilary Thompson than have a three and four year old sibling burden. But she had no choice and slowed her step for us to catch up.

"You make sure you look after them now," my mother called after her.

She did her best but sometimes a little brother's stubbornness is more than a ten-year-old sister can handle.

John asked one summer day, "Can I go in the pond?"

"No. It's too deep."

"But it's hot. I want to go in."

"No! It's too deep."

John's headstrong and rash character often found him in trouble and this occasion was one such time. He made his decision and without a backward glance he ran towards the water's edge. After a nonplussed moment, Kathleen burst into a sprint after him.

"You come back here John Toland. I'll tell Mam on you."

Enjoying the chase, John ran straight into the burn fully clothed; his shorts and multi-coloured jumper soon became sodden. The water shelved away and within a few strides his feet no longer touched the bottom and he began to flounder. The more he struggled the more his cheeky mischievous face transformed into fear and panic. Kathleen stopped motionless at the bank's edge. She watched her brother bob and splutter for seconds, for minutes she could not tell, until a deep protective instinct, motherly even, released the roots that kept her fixed to the bank. She must save her brother. Unable to swim, she took a tentative step into the pond, also fully clothed, found her balance and walked towards her brother.

She parted the water with all her strength until she reached John and dragged him back to the bank. She claimed to have been out of her depth too and has no idea how they both kept from drowning that day. Her courage meant John lived to plunge into many more scrapes.

Kathleen's biggest fear about the whole episode was how to explain to Mum why their clothes were soaking wet.

A shallow weir edged with rough stones lay beneath the bridge. Egged on by one another, we often slid down the bank and forded the width of the pond using the top of the weir as a flooded path, taking extra care on the slippery mossy parts. The pool was deep and none of us could swim having never had the opportunity to learn. None-the-less the danger from drowning was far from our minds.

We set ourselves challenges. One was to run the length of the narrow bridge parapet, which, on one side, had a drop of about ten feet to the pool. The boys skipped the span in no time, oblivious of the real danger below. I on the other hand held back. I was six years old and small for my age. To me, the water and weir were a perilously long way down. Those jagged stones that lined the edge were also a powerful deterrent. Yet, if my quest was to prove that girls were equally as brave as boys, I had at least to attempt the challenge. I mounted the parapet at one of its ends and, ignoring heckles from the boys, took a few hesitant steps forward. The sharp stones below seemed sharper still, enough to make me stop and turn around. The next time I took a few more steps and held my arms outstretched for balance. I kept my head down to concentrate hard on my feet placement, but my nerve failed once more and again I turned back. The day I walked all the way across I jumped up and down, joyous in my triumph. Yet, if I ran the length of the parapet, glory and adulation from the boys would be mine.

"Gan on, dare you. Run you chicken."

The taunts were effective and after swallowing deep gulps of courage, I ran across. From then on I found the task an easy one.

Most days after school John and I took our time to walk home. We loitered at the bridge over the Burn to delay the inescapable chores that awaited us at home. Sometimes we lingered until the school bus from Wooler dropped off our older brothers and sister at the road end, after which we walked home with them. One day, Paddy, who possessed a mean streak and enjoyed tormenting us younger ones, thought he would have some fun with John. He picked him up and dangled him over the bridge by his legs. John's face grew from pale pink to deep red as the blood rushed to his head. The more he howled and screamed the longer Paddy would dangle. Day after day this happened.

John had had enough. Determined to avoid being turned upside down ever again, he left the bridge early. He ran 'hell for leather' and had almost reached the top of the field before Paddy arrived. Phew! He had escaped. But no, Paddy ran after him and dragged him back down. How dare John deny him his bullying indulgence? Once again John wriggled and squirmed in Paddy's grasp. Paddy was nine years older and much stronger, but this time he began to lose grip of John's legs and could feel them slipping through his fingers. By the time his grip had slipped to John's ankles Paddy was trembling with fear. He was about to drop his little brother head first onto the weir; his skull might crack; he might die. The consequences were unthinkable.

Perhaps self-preservation or just sheer determination helped him somehow regain control. He tightened his hold and gradually hauled his little brother to safety. John, who seemed blessed with a 'coat of many lives', lost another that day.

Paddy received a terrible fright and never subjected John to this torture again.

The Burn was our playground through the seasons. One autumn morning a shimmering veil of mist hung over it. The trees leaves were beginning to take on the tinge of reds and golds.

John and I approached the bridge on our way to school. We spotted the creamy white chest of a weasel and watched it flash through the grass blades as it scuttled along the hedgerow hunting prey. John was by my side one moment; the next, without a hint of warning, he scrambled down the bank and pushed through the damp grass on the Burn's verge. "Come and look at this," he yelled.

A giant puffball, the size of a football, smooth and white, grew at the water's edge among the rushes. He reached out his foot to test its firmness and stepped back startled when the puffball broke apart. He lost his balance and slipped into the water. He prevented himself from being submerged altogether by clutching a handful of rushes. Before I reached the destroyed fungus he had already pulled himself out. I giggled at the drenched boy. "Eee, you're gan to be in trouble. How you gan to get dried?"

He took off his trousers, socks and shoes and I helped him squeeze as much water from them as possible. He waddled to school holding his legs wide apart, like a toddler in a full nappy. I laughed at the sight. Another life lost!

The Burn had a darker side.

John and I each had a 'pet' cat. In fact these were working cats with the job of keeping down the rat and mouse population. They were seldom given food - at the most they might be given a saucer of milk. Regarding them as 'pets' was a bit dubious, however John and I cared not for the job they had to do, to us they were our special animals. After all they spent a large part of the day asleep in warm nooks in our house. John's cat Dusty was a gentle grey female. Mine, an enormous tabby tomcat called Tiger. I loved this cat with all my heart and stroked and talked to him for hours. His patience and tolerance of me was remarkable and many times I would rouse him from sleep and dress him in my clothes: 'T' shirts, jumpers and even an old frilly frock.

He could tolerate a great deal but his patience would run out when I pretended to put him in a cot by pressing and squeezing him down the sides of the armchair. This was too much, after all he was a cat; he would lash out with his claws and scratch my arms and legs before leaping away clad in whatever outfit I'd dressed him in that day. I never learned my lesson because I would do it over and over and suffer the inevitable lacerations.

One day when I was six or seven, Tiger disappeared. I was inconsolable. Days and weeks passed with only a few reported sightings of him somewhere in the area.

I pleaded, "Mammy, Mammy, please can we go and find him."

My persistent whines and appeals drove Mum to distraction until she finally agreed and asked Kathleen, on more than one occasion, to take on the search. Kathleen never ventured far in the hunt, just far enough out of my sight to convince me she had genuinely looked for him. Each time she returned without my Tiger I became grief-stricken all over again.

No one explained to me that it was natural for un-neutered tomcats to wander, perhaps to look for a female, perhaps curious or perhaps they just lost their way. Perhaps Tiger had died.

One day, after a year had passed, I was in my bedroom dressing for school when Mum opened the door. She said, "Look who's here." I stared at the animal walking across the threshold. He looked thinner and his ear had been split in two but I knew straight away my Tiger had returned. He strode across the floor and leapt onto the bed. He rubbed his chin against my fingers demanding attention. I hugged and stroked him and held him to my face. He pressed his head into my neck and arched his back, as if in ecstasy. This could well have been his first contact with a human in a year. How I had missed his deep purrs. If anyone else went near him he hissed and bared his teeth like a wildcat. Somehow he remembered me. I would never know but perhaps the connection between us stayed in his cat memory like it had in mine.

Tiger had returned and Dusty was on heat. The inevitable happened. Some weeks later, Dusty took herself off to a barn and gave birth to four kittens. John and I wanted to keep at least one but our parents forbade it.

"If we kept every kitten born, this place would be overrun with them," Mum said. "No, you put them straight into a sack and put stones in the bottom. Make sure you tie the sack good and tight now, so they can't get out. Then throw the sack in the burn."

We stood at the pond's edge with our sack parcel weighed down with stones, not for the first time and not for the last. The newborn kittens, their eyes still shut, writhed against the sacking like sacrificial lambs. We closed our ears to the tiny mews calling for their mother. John lifted the sack above his shoulders and hauled it into the pool. We watched the water part and swallow its prize.

But, life is full of surprises. Several weeks later a stray kitten, old enough to have recently been weaned, wandered into the farm and attached itself to our household. Mum was having none of it and ordered John to take it to the Burn.

He fed the Burn another sacrifice and turned to walk away when he saw the kitten's body bob to the surface and float downstream. "How can that be?' he thought. Mystified, he shrugged his shoulders and walked on to call for Mark Thompson.

"I thought I told you to drown that kitten." Mum glared at John when he arrived home later.

"I did Mam. I chucked the sack in the Burn. I did. I saw its dead body in the water."

"Is that so," she said. "Well what is that wee thing doing there then?"

She pointed to the kitten curled up on the grass asleep. It looked so content it was hard to believe it had just survived a traumatic experience.

This miracle kitten had somehow swum free and made its way back to the farm half a mile uphill. Was the instinct to live, even in a kitten a few weeks old, truly so strong? John clearly hadn't tied the sack tight enough and the kitten had floated to the surface unconscious. After the initial shock of the water the kitten must have regained consciousness and swum to freedom.

Mum was in a forgiving mood and said we could keep it.

"By the grace of God, that wee thing was saved from the drowning. Who am I to disagree with the Lord?"

Many cats prowled the farm and kittens were being born all the time. Drowning them was normal practice and deemed a necessary cull. To this day tiny bones lay scattered at the bottom of the pond and a nasty taste of cruelty lingers on my tongue. The death of these little fur bundles was quick and clean but that is scant consolation.

The Burn was a place of fun, daring and miraculous escapes. It's a marvel we all of us survived its traps and perils throughout the years without serious injury. My mother said, "The good Lord was looking after you."

I say we were just lucky and got away with it.

# Chapter 10

# Harvest

June Fiddes and I were playing 'bays', our name for hopscotch. We chalked out ten bays on the Cement and selected our slate pieces ready for the game. I prided myself at being good at it and threw my slate into the perfect place in the number seven bay. I hopped towards it, being careful to stay within the chalk lines, when a distraction caused me to look out towards the school. It may have been the deep distant thrum of the motor or the flash of red in the corner of my eye.

"Look June," I yelled pointing towards the road end, chalk lines forgotten. "Mammy, John, come quickly."

Mum and John rushed out of the cottage, Mum's face aghast as if to say, "What now?"

"Look, see," I said. "The combines are coming."

The wheat, ripe for cutting, swayed in the breeze as the combine harvester chugged down the road in preparation for harvest.

I jumped up and down, beside myself with excitement, "The combines are coming. The combines are coming."

Every year we looked forward to harvest time when we spent hot days in the fields with the workmen. We would watch the combines close up and even sit in the driver's seat when it was stationary. The farm filled with extra labourers and the noise, the dust and the cut wheat smell added to the adventure of crop gathering. The combine itself fascinated us; huge and red like a giant prehistoric creature that clacked its jaws and rattled its armour. What a thrill to watch up close the spiky blades lower into the thick wheat and rotate as the combine moved forward slashing and devouring the crop. Rats and field mice scattered in fright. Those too slow to escape were sometimes spiked. To protect the grain from rat flesh contamination, workers walked alongside the combine with pitchforks ready to extract the unfortunate animal and cast it to the crows. The farm cats skulked along the field's edges to wait their opportunity to catch fleeing mice.

Soon several combines crept along the distant fields of neighbouring farmsteads looking like tiny red spiders.

The combine worked through the field in ruler-straight rows swallowing and digesting the cut wheat into the onboard storage container while at the same time the spent straw poured forth from the rear end. When the container became full, the grain spilled from the outstretched arm nozzle into the trailer of a waiting tractor. We ran alongside the tractor until the trailer was full and then rode atop the cargo on its way to the 'Dryer' opposite the Burn, half a mile away. A number of tractors waited in line beside the combine because it never stopped. After ours drove off fully loaded another pulled alongside to take its place.

Two large sheds housed the drying rooms. The first and older Dryer contained a conical concrete pit dug deep into the ground. The cut grain was unloaded into this pit via a chute. The grain would have been air dried here in the early days before the second shed, with its more modern drying machines, had been installed. A corkscrew-type lift at the bottom of the pit in the first shed scooped up the grain and transported it to the newer building to be dried, graded, weighed and bagged.

Our trailer backed up to the chute and the driver unlatched the tailboard. We scrambled over the grain to the back of the trailer as it winched up gradually so the wheat could cascade into the pit in a controlled manner. Our excitement mounted the higher the trailer rose. The best bit was about to happen.

"Wheeee!" We laughed and squealed as we slid from the trailer with the last of the load and landed on top of the compacted grain mound below. We lay on our backs in the pit's dim light with our arms and legs outstretched and wriggled to make star shapes in the mound. When we pulled ourselves up to stand the grain slowly filled our impressions until the stars fizzled away.

To climb out of the pit we struggled to cross the grain towards a vertical metal ladder hammered into the wall, one foot forward, two backwards like a scramble up a steep shingle slope.

The chute slide was undoubtedly a dangerous game, one we were warned against, but the tractor drivers usually turned a blind eye if the pit was at least half full; less than half would have been too dangerous for fear we might become caught up in the corkscrew lift. That roller-coaster ride, which disappeared into the darkness, was the highlight of our harvest.

Clear of its load the tractor returned to the combine ready to collect the next one, and so the process continued until each field had been shorn.

Harvest time was heavy toil for the men. They worked long shifts throughout each twenty-four hours and used up every scrap of daylight to gather in the crop, in case of a sudden change in weather. Some worked in the fields driving the tractors and others worked at the Dryer turning the grain to ensure air flowed evenly through it to prevent mould spores settling. They shovelled the dried grain into sacks. The filled sacks were taken to the granary at the farm for storage. The men would cough wheat dust from their lungs or pick it from their fingernails and ears for days afterwards.

One harvest time, Big James Collins had worked several eighteen-hour days at the Dryer. He was so exhausted it led to a serious incident with Big John Fiddes. James had submitted his weekly hours to the head office at Hetton Steads as usual. The workers enjoyed a lucrative period during harvest and looked forward to fatter wage packets. They needed some reward for the hot, tedious work and extensive overtime. This particular day, Big John Fiddes received a phone call from the office with a query over James' hours. He came up the path from his cottage and passed us children playing on the Cement.

"Where you gannin, Big John?" we asked.

Usually he would stop and joke with us or ruffle our hair but this time he paid us no attention and walked straight on to the Collins' house and knocked. Rose opened the door.

"Can a' speak to James, please?" John asked.

"He's just finished his shift and is having his tea. Can it not wait?" Rose replied.

"It won't take long.

Rose raised her eyebrows in irritation; she knew whatever he wanted could surely wait. But she relented, "Aye, al'right then."

James came to the door wiping a breadcrumb from his mouth. His eyes were heavy with fatigue. He glared at his boss with a hint of hostility, which suggested, *"Cannut a man have his tea in peace."*

John said, "I'm sorry to disturb you James but the office says you've claimed an hour too much this week."

"What! Ye disturb me tea fer that."

"I'm sorry man, but I need to explain to them why you've claimed an hour more than you've worked."

James opened his mouth in disbelief and after a few moments silence he stepped outside and pushed John in the chest, as if exhaustion had flicked a switch. He pushed him again, which caused John to stumble backward.

We stopped playing, sensing we were about to behold a drama much more interesting than our game.

James raised his bare fists and said, "Come on you bugger. Accuse me of cheating would yer?"

"Look, I'm only doing me job," said John as he stepped forward to try and reason with him. But James, pumped up with rage, had no time for reason. His face changed from pink to red as his anger increased. He lashed out with a fist. John, who was taller and lighter on his feet, sidestepped the punch with skill. Another lash, another side step, until James at last made contact. That was it. John had had enough of this unstable man. He would put an end to it. He steadied his feet and raised his own fists.

By now the adults had piled out of their cottages to spectate. My dad wore a huge grin on his face and mimed punches into the air; the brawl appealed to his combative nature. Rose urged someone to stop the fight. Jessie Fiddes rushed up the slope just in time to see her husband give James a thwack across the jaw, which sent him reeling. An "Ooof," came from the crowd at that punch. It was like watching Sugar Ray Robinson boxing with a punch bag. James was no match for the bigger man with fists alone. He picked himself up and went into the wood shed at the side of the house. Moments later he emerged with a long handled axe held above his head.

"Eee no!" said someone in the crowd. "What does he think he's gan ti dee wi that?"

Jessie slapped her hand across her mouth horrified that her husband might be split in two. June began to cry, worried for her daddy. The remainder of us children, which included James' daughters, Rosemary and Evelyn, stood open-mouthed in awe of what might happen next. I sidled over to Evelyn and slipped my hand into hers. I hoped in my small way to give her comfort.

"Come on yer bastard. See what yer can do now?"

James readied the axe and inched towards John. The fight, no longer sport for the spectators, had taken a serious turn. Someone needed to intervene.

"Give me the axe Big James."

My seventeen-year-old brother Paddy spoke these words as he walked towards him.

"Come on now man, give me the axe."

James stopped abruptly as if the sound of Paddy's calm voice pierced his rage. His face became downcast, fearful and full of shame. Like a submissive dog he cowered and allowed Paddy to take the axe from his raised grasp.

The larger, stronger adult males had stood by and let a teenage boy break up the fight.

It took guts to confront an unpredictable man wielding an axe. I felt proud of my big brother but was too young to understand how bold and courageous Paddy had been that day.

The show ended. John walked back to his home with his family and, bit-by-bit, the adults dispersed. Apart from a gash on James' cheek, the more pugnacious onlookers, like my dad, may have been a little disappointed that real blood had not been spilled. We children were left to ponder what we had just witnessed.

All because of one hour – and gruelling work.

The fields that had been lush with golden wheat were now rough with blunt stub ends and drills of loose straw. The combine harvester's work was done. Now it was the turn of a tractor towing a baling machine to traverse those same drills. The baler would suck the straw into its belly and perform a conjuring trick to deliver a neat oblong bale from its rear end tied in string. Soon the fields would be strewn with bale parcels dotted in evenly spaced rows.

One day a worker ran from the field and shouted, "Big John has lost his thumb in the baler."

John had been clearing clogged straw from the rotor rakes while the machine was still running. To save time the men sometimes judged it safe to do so without the need to stop the machine. On this occasion John judged incorrectly. His thumb became trapped and the blades severed the top half. It ended up buried somewhere in the resulting bale. Blood poured from his decapitated thumb and Jessie patched it as best she could. Someone else drove him to the hospital in Berwick for proper treatment. (This would not be the last time John lost a part of his body. Four years later he held a nail in position on a wooden post. He struck the hammer against the nail. It flew out and the sharp end buried itself into his right eye. He was flown by helicopter to Newcastle General hospital but, sadly, the doctors could not save it. My mother said, "Poor fella. That man has terrible luck." John endured his glass eye with his usual stoicism.)

The straw bales were transported to the stackyard and built into stacks. At the end of harvest ten oblong stacks, each twenty-foot high and eight feet wide filled the yard.

One of our favourite pastimes as children was to climb to the top of the stacks. Someone kept watch otherwise there would be 'hell to pay' if we were caught. That year I feared we might find Big John's thumb poking out of one of the bales, threatening, as if to say, "Caught you."

We clung to straw clumps and binder twine that held the bales together as we scrambled upwards. I found going up easy but the climb down was much more of a challenge. Atop we lay on our bellies and spied the surrounding cottages and fields. Tall trees obscured our view into the grounds of the Thompson's House but we could spy on our mothers in the garden hanging out washing or digging vegetables. We called out to them and when they turned to look in the direction of the call we dived down and lay as flat as possible hidden from view. Mum sometimes quizzed us later.

"Tell the truth now. Have you been climbing the haystacks today?"

"No Mam, we weren't."

"Well, it must have been the haystack fairies calling me then. Stay away from them, you hear me. You'll break yer necks one of these days."

"Yes Mam."

During one harvest, years earlier, when I was a baby, Paddy, Hubert and Kathleen found a wide gap in the bottom of one of the stacks big enough to allow all three of them to crawl in. They made a den.

"It's really dark and scary in here," said Kathleen.

"Shall we get a candle?" asked Hubert.

"Good idea," said Paddy. "You get the candle and a'll get the matches."

Big John Fiddes spotted them as they crawled back into the den and, before they had time to strike the match, he yelled, "Come oot o' there yer wee brats."

One by one he dragged them out. A peaceful man at heart John never raised a hand to children but he was so incensed this time he shook and slapped each of them. They flinched in silence, heads down in shame, as John lectured them on the dangers of taking matches into a stackyard, let alone a candle.

"Your owld enough to kna' better. You could have been burnt alive. Do you kna' that."

Paddy was eleven years old and certainly should have known better. Later Dad gave each a few belt lashes and Mum sent them to bed without tea.

The near escape from being burnt alive should have been a warning and a lesson.

A few years later, when I was eight years old, the community prepared to celebrate the end of harvest. The stackyard was full and the fields ready to be re-planted. Mum and I were in the Fiddeses house. I stood with June by the window next to the phone. Mum and Jessie sat by the hearth chatting and drinking tea. The afternoon sun began to lower and shadows lengthen.

I looked out of the window and saw flames suddenly flare from the stackyard and said to June, "Eee, that's a big fire."

Mum and Jessie leapt from their seats. Jessie pushed June and me out of the way of the phone and called the office in Hetton Steads to ask them to alert the fire brigade. The phone line was internal only.

The flames rose and crackled, and a million dancing sparks pirouetted higher as they waltzed to the next stack and the next. The weather had been fair for weeks and the straw was tinder dry. Each stack ignited like a giant exploding firecracker.

"Look Mammy," I said, "there's our John and Mark Thompson."

"Jesus, Mary and Joseph! Glory be to God!" These were my mother's signature words for any crisis.

The two boys rushed from the stackyard entrance clearly terrified. Mum ran to meet them and scooped John into her arms. She drew both boys away from the danger. Later John confessed he and Mark had gathered loose straw that lay on the ground and built their own miniature stack. They wanted a bonfire and put a match to it. Proud of their fire they whooped around it like Indian braves. Seconds later a spark struck the first stack nearby and set it alight.

John sobbed unable to see through his steamed up national health glasses. His tears could have been from genuine fright but more likely from the thought of the punishment he was sure to receive. Mark Thompson stood next to John dry-eyed but contrite. He slunk away to his house to await the inevitable scolding from his parents.

Word spread quickly and workers from all the surrounding farms rallied. Husbands and wives turned up on their tractors to help. The fire brigade would take at least an hour to arrive. Until then every able body formed lines and passed buckets of water taken from the spring near the stackyard and from people's houses. Men shouted instructions through the smoke filled air while the fire continued to mock the crowd with hisses and crackles. Ten stacks were alight before the fire brigade arrived. Water cascaded from the engine hoses but it soon became clear the stacks were doomed. A winter's worth of straw bedding for the cattle hemmels would soon be reduced to a fine layer of blackened cinder. Weeks of labour vanquished in minutes by the foolhardiness of youth.

A large Dutch barn full of hay stood at the edge of the stackyard. The hay was precious winter feed for the cattle. Saving it was imperative. Everyone directed their effort now at creating a firebreak between the burning stacks and the barn.

John and I were ordered to stay indoors.

"And don't ye dare come out agen. Yer've done enough damage fer one day."

'*But I didn't do anything,*' I wanted to say. How unfair and totally unjust to be included in the accusation? My dad's fierce scowl set the fear of God in us. Instead we scrunched up together on the windowsill in the corridor that led to the bedrooms and viewed the drama from there.

"It's like the biggest bonfire in the whole world," I said.

We sat goggle-eyed as the water spouted from the fire engine's hose. I knew I should be anxious for my mum and dad and the other folks fighting the blaze but the raging fire that illuminated the darkening sky, and the bustle and chaotic shouts coming from every direction filled me with thrills.

John, less enthusiastic, screwed up his face and chewed at his nails as we watched each stack burn.

"What's wrong? Why are yer pulling faces?" I asked.

"I'm scared the hay will catch light."

"Why?"

"Cos what'll the cattle eat in the hemmels if it gets burned." His voice trembled as he held back the tears. "A'll get such a leathering, a know a will."

Still the flames licked at the edge of the Dutch barn.

We were almost asleep when Mum walked into our bedroom hours later. An eerie quietness filled the room. The fire engines, the workers and wives, weary and black from soot, had returned home. Mum looked exhausted. A film of sweat coated her face and streaks of her hair clung to her flushed cheeks.

She simply said, "It's out."

John sat bolt upright, "Did they save the hay, Mam?"

"Yes, John, they did."

# Chapter 11

# The Church

"Will yous two hurry up. The Trojan will be here in a minute," Mum shouted.

Every Sunday the Trojan picked up Catholic children from around the countryside and delivered them to the Catholic Church in Lowick.

My mother fussed over us, checking my ringlets were neat and that John was wearing his glasses. As she retrieved money from her purse she said, "Have yer got yer rosary beads?"

"Yes Mam."

"Have yer got yer prayer books?"

"Yes Mam."

"Now, here's some pennies for the collection. You make sure you put them in the plate mind. Don't you go spending them on anything else."

"Yes Mam," we said, emphasizing the '*yes*' with an impatient shrug.

She went to put her purse away when she said, "Oh glory be to God, I nearly forgot. After church go to the back of Mabens and ask if they have any spare bread." Mum handed me a few more pennies.

"Ahh Mam, do I have to?

"Will yer wheesht yer mouth. We need the bread."

"But why's it always me who has to do it?" Despite my protests I pocketed the pennies all the same.

Mabens were the bakers in Lowick. They baked on the premises and made van deliveries to the CWS farms twice a week. Every now and then my hungry family had eaten all our bread by Saturday evening. Never to waste an opportunity, Mum insisted we, no I, knock on Maben's back door and disturb their Sunday morning. Sometimes the baker had loaves left over from the Saturday batch, which they sold off cheap to anyone cheeky enough to bother them.

John and I ran from the cottage and down the slope to the farmyard to wait for the Trojan. We joined the four Collins children, Rosemary and Evelyn, Little James and Anthony, and two new Italian children, Marie and Tony Gavioli. The Gaviolis had recently moved into the middle cottage when I was seven. Their parents, Charlie and Nanda, spoke broken English with a strong accent and I struggled to understand what they said. They were kind people and Marie and Tony became our friends. They lived on the farm for a year before moving away.

We clambered aboard the Trojan and jostled for seats. Three children from neighbouring farms were already on board. I managed to squeeze between Rosemary and Evelyn, eager to stay close to my best friends.

The Trojan was about the size of a Transit van and had a quirky shape. It had a black and brown exterior and the interior had hard uncomfortable side bench seats. Back and side windows gave us a view of the countryside, not that we saw much with all the fooling around that took place. Every time the vehicle drove over a road bump we would be lifted from our seats to plonk down again amongst giggles and snorts. Turning corners was worse – either we were at risk of being thrown across the aisle to land in the opposite traveller's lap or, if we sat at the row's end, squashed against the back window or the front seat like a closing concertina of children.

The Trojan trundled along the narrow roads, passed Hetton Law and onto the Roman road, called 'Devil's Causeway' that led all the way to Lowick, seven miles north. Once there, we piled out and dragged our feet up the church path to delay as long as possible the ordeal of the Mass. I hated church. John and I were the only members of my family forced to attend. Paddy lived at home but was considered an adult and spared. Hubert had left home to join the Royal Navy as a cadet; Joe and Kathleen had already been confirmed so were also spared. Neither did my parents attend, so why did John and I have to?

"Because there isn't room in the Trojan for all the adults as well," my mother replied. "Sure, we pray to the Lord in different ways. I say my prayers to Him every day." She pointed to the dreaded picture of Jesus Christ that hung above the mantelpiece, His exposed 'sacred heart' wrapped in a crown of thorns dripping with blood.

I thought they should just buy a bigger Trojan.

The unfathomable Latin Mass seemed interminable. The pews and kneelers were made of hard wood and we had to kneel - a **lot**. What a relief when Father Corrigan began the blessing – the service would soon be over.

After Mass I ran to Mabens. I could feel my throat stiffen with tension as I knocked on the back door. I prayed this would be one of Mrs Maben's 'happy' days.

When she opened the door the wonderful baking aroma filled my senses. Fresh buttered bread and jam images made me forget for a moment why I stood outside the bakers; but only for a moment. Mrs Maben glowered before me. She tilted her head to one side and frowned down her nose. "Is that you again, Margaret Toland?" It wasn't a question.

"My Mam says have you got a spare white loaf please?" I could hear a voice squeak out the words, tiny and far away, as if it belonged to someone else.

"What did you say? I cannut hear you."

She heard me the first time of course but I repeated the request, louder this time.

"You need to tell your mother she should buy more from the van when it comes round."

Mrs Maben tutted and went inside to fetch the bread. So much for my prayers - she was having a cranky day. She clearly would have preferred to be left in peace on her day off. I felt so embarrassed I could feel the prickles of pinkness creep into my face and neck. Mrs Maben returned with the loaf and I handed her the pennies.

"Don't forget to tell your mother now." Her words echoed down the street as I clutched the day-old bread and ran back to the Trojan.

The hostile stares from the children eager to get home, get changed and out to play, added to my humiliation. I avoided their gaze as I eased myself onto the bench next to John.

I whispered to him, "You can gan next time. It's your turn."

Every Sunday through the seasons the Trojan carried us to church. One day, when I was eight, news came that the vehicle had broken down irreparably and would not be replaced. This delicious information meant we would no longer have to attend church in Lowick. While I was jubilant at leaving behind the red-rubbed knees, the baffling mumbles of the priest and the knocking on back doors, I would miss the fun Trojan trips because I rarely had the opportunity to ride aboard any vehicle.

My euphoria was short-lived. More news arrived that Father Corrigan, a cantankerous man who had little patience with anyone, was to be replaced by a Father Devlin.

Father Corrigan had cared little that a significant number of his flock from the outer regions never attended church; the fewer people, the fewer confessions he had to listen to and the sooner he could have an afternoon nap.

Father Devlin on the other hand, cared deeply for his parishioners and was dismayed that, in particular, children were being deprived of God's grace. We were too young yet to be sinners but we still needed to be bathed in His love. Father Devlin fretted for his absent congregation and determined to bring God to us.

This was terrible news. Father Devlin had a car and each Sunday, directly after he took Mass in Lowick, he would drive to our house where he conducted Mass all over again. The adults now had no excuse. They too would be obliged to attend Mass.

On these occasions Father Devlin would bring a suitcase full of the necessary religious trappings that would turn our kitchen table into an altar. Dad would pull the table from the back wall into the middle of the room, which left enough space behind for the priest and in front for the small congregation.

Father Devlin dressed the table with a white cloth and then placed a sparkling silver chalice in the middle. He folded another smaller white cloth and draped it gently across the chalice top. He removed two tall candles in silver candlesticks from his case and put these either side of the chalice. At the end of the table he placed two small glass vessels, one contained holy water and the other wine. Beside these he laid a paten, the silver plate that would hold the Eucharist bread, in preparation for anyone who wished to receive Holy Communion. The last and most important, he placed his bible in front of the chalice. The altar was complete.

Meanwhile Mum and Dad tidied themselves up. Dad smothered his hair in Brylcreem and sleeked it back with a comb. Mum dabbed on powder and red lipstick. To lessen the brightness of the red she took a piece of toilet paper, folded it in half, placed it between her lips and pressed down. I loved to watch her and unconsciously pressed my own lips together in mimicry. A perfect imprint daubed the paper and her lips transformed from garish to muted. She then brushed the paper lightly across her cheeks with the smudged lipstick to create a pink blush. She changed from 'everyday' into 'beautiful'.

The Collinses and Gaviolis arrived in their Sunday best. They brought kitchen chairs to sit on and rolled up towels to kneel on; our stone floor was even harder than the wooden church kneelers. The chairs were laid out in neat rows and our living room transformed into a miniature church.

Everyone crowded in front of the altar and Father Devlin, dressed in his priest's robes, conducted the Mass rites and liturgies beneath the image of Jesus Christ.

In the confined space our small congregation stood, sat and knelt as the Mass progressed. Low, monotonic voices droned in unison the Latin responses to the priest's instructions:

Priest: *Dominus vobiscus*    *(The Lord be with you)*
Us: *et cum spiritu tuo*    *(And with your spirit)*
Priest:*Kyrie eleison*    *(Lord have mercy)*
Us: *Kyrie eleison*
Priest: *Christie eleison*    *(Christ have mercy)*
Us: *Christie eleison*

And all the while, Jesus looked down from His picture frame, watchful, and His open heart bled.

Ash Wednesday dawned and Lent began, six weeks before Easter Sunday: time to emulate the Son of God and fast for forty days. Father Devlin dipped his thumb in a small round dish that contained ash from the burnt palm crosses from the previous year. A fresh set of palm crosses, reputedly made from dried palm fronds, would be distributed to each parishioner on Palm Sunday and collected afterwards. These would be saved and later burnt for the following year's Ash Wednesday.

"Remember, you came from dust and to dust you will return," the priest intoned as he raised his thumb and marked each of our foreheads with the ash in the sign of a cross.

Proud of my black mark I showed it off to June Fiddes.

"I wish I could have one," she said, examining my forehead.

But June was not a Catholic and the priest told me Catholics were God's chosen people and only we were special enough to receive the mark.

I enjoyed her envy and ensured mine stayed in place the entire day.

Young children were not expected to fast but encouraged instead to 'give up' something for the duration; something we would miss and yearn for, not something we were indifferent to. Most years we chose 'sweets'. Each week when the grocery van called at the farm Mum allowed us to choose a halfpenny packet of toffees or chews. John and I saved these packets in our personal biscuit tins. We hid our tins from one another to avoid any temptation to thieve. I counted my booty regularly to ensure my brother had not been seduced. Sometimes visitors brought us a sherbet tube or chocolate, or a lollipop. These too would be deposited in the tin. Self-restraint was a hard lesson to learn and many a time my hand would hover over the lid ready to sneak a toffee. *Surely one tiny sweet won't count,* I told myself, but the terrifying thought of burning in hell for my sin triumphed over temptation every time.

The long six weeks of Lent at last came to an end on Easter Sunday. Self-restraint crumbled into the dust I had come from. I sat on the floor with my tin in my lap and gorged on sweets and chocolates until my mother took the tin away saying, 'That's enough for one day."

John and I had reached the age to take our first Holy Communion. I was eight and he, nine. To be worthy of the privilege, our hearts and minds had to be prepared for our 'first confession'. Since we were unable to go to Sunday school Father Devlin stayed behind after Mass at our house to give us catechism lessons. He provided us with a copy of the text to share and for homework each week, set us a series of questions about the Catholic doctrine to which we had to learn the answers, by heart.

The catechism passages were intensely dull but we were good Catholic children and committed every verse to memory. We tested each other ready for the next session. Sibling rivalry meant we worked hard at memorizing the answers to see who could impress Father Devlin the most.

Our first confession was the worst part of the whole preparation. The priest had a moral imperative to cleanse our young souls before we took the holy Eucharist. In normal circumstances the sinner would sit in a dark confessional box in church with the priest behind a meshed screen, anonymous, neither one able to see the other.

Not so for John and me. Father Devlin did not have a confessional box tucked inside his suitcase. Instead, he sat on a chair in one of our bedrooms, side on, and asked that we pretend he sat behind a screen. I had a lively imagination but this was farcical. I knelt before the chair and said, "Bless me father for I have sinned..." and proceeded to confess my sins, deeply humiliated and ashamed.

After the priest's absolution however, I said my 'Hail Marys' penance and, absolved of guilt and sin, felt squeaky clean.

This confessional took place on a Saturday in late spring 1959. The next day John and I truly believed we would receive Christ's body and blood for the first time. The day broke and the sun rose to fill the air with warmth. The pristine blue sky bowed its head as if to acknowledge the purity of what we were about to receive.

I jumped out of bed highly excited.

"Get up John. It's morning. It's our first Holy Communion today."

I ran to Mum. "Mam, Mam. Can I get dressed now? Please!"

"No you cannut, not yet. Yer'll only get yer dress dirty."

My new dress and veil hung in the wardrobe. I gazed at the white satin, white to signify purity and beauty of soul. It had a frill across the chest, a Peter Pan collar and a broad satin belt tied in a bow at the back. The soft, silky fabric slithered through my fingers and I could hardly wait to wear it.

I tried to keep myself occupied but every five minutes found myself at the wardrobe drooling, until at last the time came. I put on my dress, white socks and white shoes. Mum tied my belt and then attached the veil to the crown of my head. It hung long and shimmered over my neatly curled ringlets. Never before had I worn anything as enchanting. I swirled in circles just to hear the satin rustle. I pranced and danced around the kitchen and thought how fine I looked, completely ignoring the teaching that 'pride' is a sin. I was a little bride, and indeed would soon become Christ's bride - the symbolism could not be clearer.

The Holy Communion service was to take place at the Catholic Church in Lowick. Several children were being initiated at the same time and the area Bishop was to conduct the service. I cannot recall how we travelled to church, but I know my mother accompanied us. Congregation spilled from the church pews, due in part to proud parents attending; keen to watch their little ones receive the greatest gift, but mostly to revere the Bishop in his vestment finery. His visits to the Lowick church were rare and everyone wanted to see him.

"Now, when you go up, remember to genuflect in front of Our Lord before kneeling at the altar." My mother shared our nervousness and rehearsed over and over what we should do.

"And remember to say 'Thank you' at the end."

"Yes Mam."

I followed John down the aisle; our heads bowed and hands in the prayer position. I thought every pair of eyes in that church concentrated on me alone, waiting for me to stumble or make a mistake.

They waited less than a minute. I forgot to genuflect. I realised just before I took up my position at the altar. In a panic, thinking God would surely punish me to hell I stepped backward and bumped into the girl behind; she had remembered her genuflection. By now I could feel my cheeks burn and imagined it a post-box red that would have contrasted starkly with my dress and veil. Mortified I raised my forefinger to my forehead, made a rapid sign of the cross and muttered, "In the name of the Father, the

Son and the Holy Ghost, Amen." I curtsied in front of the huge crucifix that loomed high behind the altar before again joining the row of kneeling boys and little Christ brides.

Like newborn chicks in the nest we each lifted our chins, opened our mouths, stuck out our tongues, and waited.

"Corpus Christi." *(The body of Christ)*, said the Bishop as he placed a sliver thin disc, His body, on the waiting child's tongue, followed by a sip of wine, His blood.

The Bishop moved along the row at snail's pace.

"Corpus Christi."

"Corpus Christi."

At last, my turn next. I stuck out my tongue.

"Corpus Christie," said the Bishop. I felt the wafer's dryness and wondered vaguely how I would ever swallow it. Somehow I sipped the wine - or might it have been grape juice. Then I had an epiphany - inside my mouth His body and His blood were blending together to become whole. The wafer softened and Jesus Christ slid down my throat.

I said, "Thank you," and stood up from the altar. I walked back to my mother, my face restored to its normal colour. My heart felt like it had grown twice its size. [9]

9 I had no notion at such an impressionable age that as the years passed different influences would cause me to reflect long and hard about God, the church and religion; that I would reject theism and never again receive the leavened bread and wine - for that is all it was.

# Chapter 12

# Hazelrigg School

I came to.

A circle of children peered down at me each showing a mixture of concern and curiosity. Mrs Wright's face joined them and in my confused state I thought, '*What a huge face she has.*' For a few moments I wondered why I lay on the ground. Then, I felt the pain.

During that lunch break I had stood at one end of the beam, another girl stood at the other. About the height and width of a gym horse the beam was bolted into the playground. We used it for PE and at playtimes. The girl and I walked towards one another, arms outstretched, carefully balanced. We met in the middle and as we pressed our bodies together to negotiate the crossover, I overbalanced and lost my footing. Or had she pushed me? My head hit the hard concrete and I sank into unconsciousness.

Mrs Wright helped me to my feet while I tried desperately to keep back my tears. I suffered a nasty bump on the back of my head but I could speak and walk, so my teachers thought it unnecessary to send me to hospital to check if I had concussion or a cracked skull. Everyone wanted to feel my bump and despite the pain, I felt like a hero.

Hazelrigg Primary School sat on a rise a mile from Hetton Hall. The school serviced all the farms in the vicinity. The

109

building consisted of just two classrooms. Mrs Wright taught infants in the smaller room and her husband, Mr Wright, the headmaster, taught juniors in the other larger room. Class sizes were no greater than fifteen with pupils of different ages and abilities in each. The teachers split their time between the younger and older children. One set worked quietly while the teacher held a lesson with the other set. After a period the roles were swapped. As a younger junior I eavesdropped the older children's lessons and thought their work sounded much more interesting than practising letters.

The large classroom doubled up as a dining room. The desks were situated furthest away from the entrance and the dining tables closest to it. A corridor led from the classrooms to the kitchen where, each day, Mrs Gladstone cooked a hot meal. I had free school dinners, one less meal my parents needed to provide. Meat was almost always on the menu, which could not be guaranteed at home. The whole school lined up by the kitchen door to receive their dinner. A grumpy, surly woman, Mrs Gladstone grumbled and moaned as she filled our plates from large saucepans on the range. Woe betide anyone who turned up his or her nose at the food otherwise they were condemned to the fussy-faddy table - a name and shame table.

Friday was a meat free day to oblige the few Catholic children at the school. Fish often replaced meat on the menu. Father Devlin warned, "It's a venial sin to eat meat on a Friday." We were told over and over. "They crucified Our Lord on that day." If we ate meat it would be tantamount to eating Him. Yet to eat his wafer formed flesh when receiving Holy Communion was perfectly acceptable. And wasn't fish also flesh? Confused, I failed to see the difference.

I hated fish - the smell turned my stomach. Each Friday I sat at the fussy-faddy table, unabashed.

I never refused dessert since we rarely had pudding or cake at home. Rice pudding, semolina, tapioca, I devoured them all and the thicker the skin the better. One year, to my delight, Anne Wright the headmaster's daughter, invited me to her birthday party. Cake, buns and jellies decked the tea table. I could barely keep my hands from straying before being invited to sit. I tasted ice cream for the first time; milk crystals in the depths of winter were the closest I ever got to taste frozen food.

Mrs Wright placed a bowl of jelly in front of me and added a scoop of this cold whiteness. I lifted the spoon to my lips and took the teeniest taste - just in case - but when it melted and curled around my tongue, the creamy sweet deliciousness was like nothing I had ever tasted. When Mrs Wright offered a second helping I accepted without hesitation.

The Wrights owned a refrigerator - an appliance that, in our house, was years away. To keep milk from souring in the summer months Mum would stand the milk jug in a bowl of cold water and drape a muslin cloth over its top ensuring the ends of the cloth dipped into the water. The muslin soaked up the liquid and the ensuing evaporation cooled the milk. The method worked to an extent but I remember many a white fat globule of 'turning' milk floating on the surface of my tea or cornflakes.

Apart from a grassy patch the size of a tennis court, farmers' fields came right up to the school boundary. The boys played football on the grass and, in the summer months, everyone played rounders. Most other exercise took place on the concrete playground. The toilet block, located in the playground around the corner from the kitchen, consisted of two outside cubicles and an adjoining six-foot high, uncovered L-shaped urinal. The boys used this all year round, whatever the weather. They regularly held competitions to see who could pee the highest. One or two of them could reach over the wall. We girls soon learned to stand well away for fear of a 'yellow' shower.

In my first year at school I was fearful of Mr Wright. On my second day, during assembly, he announced an instruction I failed to hear. At playtime I ran over to a ladder, painted black, leaning against the wall, gripped the sides and stepped onto the bottom rung. Mr Wright came upon me in an instant. He pulled me to the side and muttered something about not paying attention in assembly and told me to wait there. My hands, dress and shoes were smeared with black paint dots. He came back a few moments later clasping a ruler and ordered me to hold out my hand. I obeyed, frightened, unaware of what I had done wrong. Children stopped their play to gloat; glad that it was not they receiving the punishment.

My hand stung from the three ruler raps and I learnt that day that teachers were always right, even when they weren't. I sobbed at the injustice and went to the cloakroom to wash off the paint. Later I found myself in trouble all over again from Mum for ruining my clothes.

Mr Wright had a cruel streak and was quick to brandish his ruler or cane. One day he was in a particularly foul mood and picked on a boy who lived at North Hazelrigg. The boy's family lacked personal hygiene and often smelled of unwashed bodies and clothes. Mr Wright had been giving a lesson in cleanliness and, to illustrate a point, pulled the boy to the front of the classroom. He ordered him to take off one of his shoes and socks. We sat alert, curious to see what would happen next. The young man's bare foot was black with dirt. Mr Wright then ordered my brother John to come to the front and remove his shoe and sock. He told both boys to stand side by side.

Mr Wright addressed the class. "Now that is a clean foot," he said pointing to John's, "Whereas that one is a disgrace."

The boy hung his head, ashamed in front of the entire class. Mr Wright was not finished with him yet. He took hold of the boy's earlobe and dragged him along the front row desks and urged each child to take a look at the muck inside his ear - then compare it to John's clean one. John squirmed with embarrassment at being held up as a shining example. He hated to be the centre of attention and was anxious to get back to his seat. The boy slunk back and slouched low in his seat trying to become invisible.

When Mr Wright raised his voice, his stern and authoritarian manner caused all children to tremble with fear. However this was meek when compared to the terror of a visit from the NHS dentist. The dentist parked his mobile unit in the playground and we stood in line to wait our turn to step inside a 'cell' full of torture implements. I became more fretful as each child in front entered and emerged from the van clutching at his or her cheek. When June Fiddes stepped out, her mouth dripped blood and spittle from a dark gap in her gum. Her clenched fist held a white tissue folded into a neat parcel. Inside was her extracted tooth. The poor girl was inconsolable and cried all afternoon. The child next in line must have been terrified.

Provided basic Maths and English were taught our headmaster had the freedom to choose the other subjects that made up the curriculum. Mr Wright's preferences were music and handwriting. Why teach academic subjects to rural kids who had little or no ambition and were destined for farm work? None would pass the 11+ so why expend effort on irrelevant subjects? [10] I had aptitude and wanted to learn but instead I spent hours practising handwriting. We were issued with calligraphy pencils. I took great care to keep my letters between the spaces of the specially lined paper. It had to slant to the right, a torment for the left-handed children. I liked the calligraphic effect the pencil created and when good enough I progressed to using a calligraphy pen and ink. Each year Mr Wright submitted handwriting samples to the county competition and I won prizes on several occasions - half-a-crown one year for first prize in my age group, a great deal of money to a child in those days. I never got to spend it as it went straight into my mother's purse. [11]

Every day John and I walked to school and took short cuts across the fields. Only in the severest winter weather, when snowdrifts had cut off the farm, were we excused from the daily trek. One winter Dad helped Big John Fiddes attach a makeshift snow plough to the front of the tractor, which they used to drive a channel through the drifts, wide

---

10 This upset me more than I realised at the time and has stayed with me my whole life.

11 If Mr Wright thought academic subjects were a waste of time then so was my pretty handwriting. I had little use for it as a skill in later life.

enough for the Hetton Hall and North Hazelrigg children
to walk to school. The drifts were higher than the hedges.
I imagined I walked through a gleaming crystal tunnel. Mr
and Mrs Wright lived in a bungalow across the playground
so were able to conduct lessons to a skeleton class. No school
bus meant no school for the farm children further afield and
no school for my older brothers and sister who attended
the secondary at Wooler.

"It's not fair," I complained to Mum. " Why de we have
to gan to school? We want to go sledging and play in the
snow too. It's just not fair."

Half an hour later I sat in a cold classroom learning my
times tables.

In June 1958 Mr Wright announced we could all look
forward to a special school trip. It had to be a very special
occasion for Hazelrigg School to organise one at all. The
young Queen Elizabeth was to visit Lindisfarne, Holy Island
and we were to go there to welcome her. As the day of the
trip approached excitement charged the playground. The
idea of Holy Island had always enchanted me. Surrounded
by water with white sand and dunes, a real castle and a
ruined priory, what could be more like a fairy-tale to a child
whose universe consisted of a farm, a church and a school?

Children and teachers piled onto a bus, which drove
us ten miles to the start of the metalled causeway that
separated Holy Island from the mainland. Twice a day
the North Sea tide swept through at speed making the
causeway impassable. A shed on stilts stood part way along;
a refuge for stranded motorists, of which there had been
several. The notion of becoming trapped thrilled me, but

then I thought, *'The shed is far too small to hold us all,'* and dismissed the image. I have no recollection as to why the bus parked at the start of the causeway and did not follow the other vehicles that drove all the way to the island.

Thirty children and two teachers disembarked and stood at the edge, awestruck at the shimmering expanse of sands and mudflats. The majority of us had never experienced such vastness. The smell of the sea hung heavy, pungent and salty. I could taste it. We had eight hours to walk across the mudflats, see the Queen and walk back before the tide returned.

Someone shouted, "You can see the castle. Look!"

It was an unimpressive craggy rock on the horizon no larger than the rocks strewn about us. I longed to reach the island to see its full size. As instructed by Mr Wright we took off our socks and shoes and tied the laces together. We hung them around our necks and stepped barefoot onto the sand. Like scuttling beetles we trailed behind our teachers for the three-mile hike. We took the ancient Pilgrim's Way, a more direct route to the Priory and further than the causeway. This kept us a safe distance from the busy traffic - much busier than usual that day in light of the special event. A line of marker posts indicated the route of the Pilgrim's Way. The posts stretched to vanishing point and the distance appeared to go on forever.

At first I found the walk exciting. I splashed through the puddles and enjoyed the sensation of cool, muddy sand and seaweed tentacles squeezing between my toes. Some boys chased tiny crabs before they escaped down holes. But soon the puddles became tedious and the distance left to walk never appeared to diminish; the trek lost its joy.

The Royal Yacht was anchored off the coast of the island but a sea mist shrouded it from view. As we walked passed post after post, the mist receded, the ship became visible and the weather became hot. I kept a watchful eye out to sea wary that the tide might unexpectedly rush in. We trudged on and still the marker poles disappeared from view. I trod on a sharp seashell and cried out. No one cared. The heat caused everyone to fade, like wilted flowers. We just wanted to get there.

Mr Wright tried to lift our spirits by explaining the history of St Cuthbert, a hermit and later bishop of Lindisfarne Priory. He said we walked in the footsteps of pilgrims who came to worship at St Cuthbert's shrine from as far back as the seventh century. By the time we reached the island my face was burned pink by the hazy sun and I was tired of St Cuthbert.

Mr and Mrs Wright shepherded us to a roped off area, which led to the Priory ruins. A colourful crowd had gathered to await Her Royal Highness. I stared dumbstruck at the ancient walls - tall, dominating - and wondered vaguely why they were tumbling down.

At last she arrived. She wore a flowery dress and a plain blue silky coat. The Duke of Northumberland walked by her side. He wore a uniform festooned with braid and medals. Prince Philip, in a dark suit, walked behind with the Duchess of Northumberland. I didn't understand why we had to wave flags and cheer the lady in the flowery dress. She meant nothing to me and I thought my mother prettier. She passed us by, waved her white, gloved hand and then she was gone. We'd had a long, hot walk for a few seconds close up.

Someone said, "Can we go and see the castle now sir?"

The answer, "No." The castle stood a mile further along the headland past the sand dunes; too far to walk before the incoming tide would cut off the island. My fairy-tale splintered. The opportunity to see a real castle for the first time blew away with the splinters to disperse among the sand dunes. When would I ever have another chance?

Like a frustrated sheepdog Mrs Wright corralled us in the village square and counted heads as we gathered.

"Where is Evelyn Collins? And where is John Toland?" She glared at me as if I was responsible for my missing brother. Mr Wright asked if anyone saw them wander off.

"No sir."

"No sir."

And so it continued. The pair had vanished. Mr Wright, clearly annoyed, set off in search. He melded into the crush of visitors who were heading towards the shore by the Lighthouse Station; their last chance to view the queen as she boarded the Royal Barge that would take her back to the Royal Yacht. Mrs Wright fussed around the rest of us and ensured no one else took it upon him or herself to wander off.

Our headmaster returned with Evelyn but without my brother. I couldn't tell if Evelyn's pink cheeks were from embarrassment or from sunburn. She wore a mischievous grin and hardly seemed aware of the anxiety she had been causing.

What had become of John? Evelyn said she had gone to look for shells by herself. I became fretful. What if he was lost forever? What if he tried to find his own way home and became caught in the tide and drowned? I was close to tears. Holy Island village was small but compared to Hetton Hall John would have found the array of buildings, churches and streets bewildering.

I sensed alarm between Mr and Mrs Wright. A missing child and the threat of a returning tide was a crisis they could do without. By now the crowds had thinned and minutes passed. Someone shouted, "Look sir, there he is." There was no mistaking the white blonde hair. John walked towards us from the direction of the priory, his face a scarlet beacon flushed with relief. I stayed close to him on the walk back across the sands. He had become distracted and when he looked up, found himself alone. He tried to catch up but became lost among the crowd. John had been frightened that day although he never admitted it.

School was a happy time for me. I loved lessons and music. I learned how to make sense of the tadpoles on sheet music, and learnt to play the recorder. We sang a lot and listened to BBC schools radio. On extremely cold winter days we huddled around the wood-burning potbelly stove at the far end of the classroom to receive our lessons. The damp wool smell pervaded the air as steam rose from the hats and gloves that dried around it. Crates of third-pint milk bottles, our daily ration, frozen from the overnight frost, stood in front of the stove to thaw.

Spring brought egg decoration and maypole dancing; summer, gingham dresses, nature rambles and flower pressing; autumn, conker fights, and winter, nativity plays where, with my blond curls, I was cast as an angel every time. Winter also brought treacherous snow and ice. One year we created an ice slide from one edge of the playground to the other. Opaque to begin with it took on a mirror-like sheen after it had been ridden time after time. Even Mr Wright showed his human side and took a turn. I stood in line with everyone else and skated to the other side but I lost my nerve when the slide became translucent, like water. Children slithered and tumbled on the glossy surface and suffered nothing worse than a bruised bum.

Tucked somewhere within those activities I learned to read, write and do arithmetic.

# Chapter 13

# Mum and Dad

My father and mother - Pat and Sadie - married in 1940. He was 22 and she 18. They possessed such different characters it's a wonder they got together at all.

Dad had a classic Celtic frame, a long back and short legs. When he sat he appeared taller, disguising a short five feet seven stature. His thin, wiry frame belied a physical strength. His blue eyes, small mouth and distinctive nose with nostrils that flared, hardly made for aristocratic features, but he had a craggy, weather-beaten handsome look all the same. While at work on the farm he wore a frayed cloth cap. On pub nights he smothered his mousey coloured hair with Brylcreem, which turned it several shades darker.

Dad's temperament was complex: he had intelligence, charm and wit, all of which were in abundance when visitors called but in short supply with his family. To us he presented a 'hard man' façade; the patriarch who must be obeyed. His patience and tolerance toward us children was volatile. He believed indulgence should be discouraged hence his cuddles were rationed. "None of this mollycoddling rubbish. It's a hard world out there. They need toughening up," he said.

He kept his weaknesses tucked away and rarely showed his vulnerability, certainly not to his children. Sometimes it felt like his personality had split in two – look away for a moment and his mood could change to a fiery temper without warning.

Yet when in good humour, Dad dropped his 'hard man' façade. He played card games or draughts with us, or picked up his button-keyed accordion and sang songs, or tussled and wrestled us. I loved it when he came home happy. I absorbed this mood like a sponge in water, as if I couldn't get enough of it, which in truth I couldn't.

His mood changes were unpredictable and I can remember quite clearly being the focus of one of those changes. He came home from work one day wearing a wide cheerful smile. This promised to be a fun evening. He sang a rude ditty that made us laugh. He then went to the bathroom to wash off the farmyard grime. He came back into the living room, stripped to his vest and was drying the back of his neck with a towel. Mum knelt by the fire poking at the coals. John pushed a toy car along the stone floor. I jumped around the room, chattering non-stop. I talked incessantly. "Twenty to the dozen," my mother said. I had many questions and plenty to tell the world. I needed a stage and audience. On this evening Dad tolerated me for a considerable time but his good mood gradually dissolved as he listened to my endless nattering. Eventually, he'd had enough of little girl nonsense. He said, "If you don't stop yer yabbering I'm going to stuff this towel down yer throat." I didn't stop. He removed the towel from around his neck, took hold of my head and started to force it into my mouth, bit by bit.

"Now will yer stop your blethering?" I felt sure I would choke and nodded my head in meek submission, trying to hold back the tears.

Another evening he came in from work and challenged John and me to a boxing match. We donned boxing gloves and punched his hard muscular frame with no impact. He laughed and teased us; said we could never be a match for him. We laughed back and punched harder. Eventually Mum sent us to the bathroom to wash and ready ourselves for bed. We'd had fun with Dad and felt happy. We splashed water at each other and created mayhem. Twice Mum came into the bathroom and warned us to behave and to be sure to wash behind our ears, but still we fooled around. Dad was in a good mood after all - he wouldn't mind. The next instant he barged into the bathroom, his expression full of rage.

"Do as your mother says, yer wee brats."

He took off his belt and wrapped it three times around his hand. Dumbfounded at the sudden change in his temper my eyes locked on the leather strap. I shivered in terror - the buckle end dangled beneath his hand. He was going to strap us with the sharp, metal buckle! We both cowered and held our arms about our heads, and waited. The thwack came, once on John's legs and once on mine. The sting made us cry out but the pain was much less than expected. Dad had changed his mind, turned the belt around and used the softer leather end instead. He perhaps never intended to use the buckle, rather he wanted to frighten us into behaving in future and do as our mother told us. Mum hovered in the background, her face full of pity, but she did not intervene. She scooped us up after the punishment and took us to bed wrapped in her hugs.

Mum's temperament was entirely different. What we lacked in cuddles from Dad we got in armfuls from her. She was easy-going, gentle and calm; full of love and warmth.

Her generous mouth always held a smile and a tune. I loved to listen to her mellow contralto voice. I often challenged her to sing a song using a word of my choice. However many words I threw at her, even the longest and hardest I could think of, she had a song in an instant. I marvelled at her ability to recall so many different melodies.

When she first came to England she would sometimes take the bus into Berwick to browse the shops she could not afford to buy from. Her natural friendliness meant she would greet strangers in the street with a smile and a, 'hello'. She was bemused by their responses as they thought her very odd. Northern folk were naturally friendly too but in the busy streets of a town it was just not practical to hail every passerby. At times like this she pined for her beloved Malin Head where no one thought it peculiar to say 'hello' to a stranger.

Her hearty laugh was her signature characteristic. She laughed often. She would fill her lungs, throw back her head, clasp her hands to her chest, open her mouth wide and expel an outrageous cackle that echoed through the air. Her laughter affected the dourest person; even they could not help but chuckle along with her.

Mum stood tall and slim and had soft brown eyes. Her thick dark hair fell in waves and framed her face. She rarely changed her hairstyle and every morning would wet it and shape the waves at the front with a comb and her fingers.

She maintained her elegant stature even after giving birth to six children. Many compliments came her way, "How do yer stay so slim and youthful Sadie?" or "When are yer gan to start ageing like the rest of us?" She shrugged off the comments beneath a veneer of modesty, but deep down enjoyed the flattery.

Yet, inside the privacy of her own living room these same people did not see her pick her nose, or spit into the fire.

"Sure, why would I dirty a clean hanky when there's a good fire blazing to burn it away."

On cold days she stood in front of the fire, facing outward and hitched up her skirt from behind to expose her stockings and knickers.

"Ooo, its lovely to warm yer backside on a day like this."

There she stayed, blocking the heat from the rest of us as she warmed the backs of her legs and bottom until her skin mottled with the heat and her veins stood out like a network of chains. She did this so often her skin became permanently mottled. Hardly elegant.

None-the-less, to me she was perfect; a saint. While I could take the chastisement and belt lashing from Dad as punishment and bounce back quickly, the cool detachment of disappointment from Mum hurt the most. One look from her made me crumble into remorse. Like the time I told her about the rat in the stackyard...

...One day, soon after the stackyard fire June Fiddes ran up the slope and shouted, "Margaret, Margaret, come and look. There's a rat in the stackyard. It's just lying there. It's not dead tho'. My mam says we should all get sticks and kill it."

The four of us; June, her brother Little John, my brother John and I, all armed with sticks, circled the rat. It lay on the ground on its side, its open eye full of fear. It twitched and shivered and clearly had only a short time to live as the poison did its work. But we came with a purpose and raised our arms one after the other and struck down on the beleaguered creature as hard as we were able. Strike after strike. Its flesh rippled after each blow. A frenzy took a grip of us all; almost lustful. The rat no longer breathed but we could not stop beating.

Our brutal streak extended to tormenting the farm cats. The boys would give chase and pick them up by their tails and throw them into the nettle patch. We laughed at their wailing screeches as they flew through the air and then scrambled from the stinging leaves. I loved animals, especially my cat Tiger and made sure the boys left him alone, but with the other cats I watched them lob and took the same pleasure it offered...

...My mother listened as we recounted the rat tale. Her face changed from cheery to downcast to sad. How could her two youngest be so pitiless? Her voice, soft and gentle, said, "It's a disgrace what you did. You know, life on the farm is hard and sometimes it means we have to kill the rats, but there is no way in this world you need to be cruel when doing it. Sure, yer wouldn't like me to beat you with a stick over and over, would yer?"

John and I were full of shame. The guilt at our mother's unhappiness outweighed a hundred times the thrill we gained from torturing animals. From that day we left the cats alone and never again lifted a stick with murderous intent.

My mother's culinary skills were limited to basic dishes, which is hardly surprising since the ingredients at her disposal were also limited. Our meals consisted of vegetables, potatoes and gravy, without variation. If we were lucky we might be given a slice of bacon or a small portion of mince or rabbit, but the lion's share of the meat was reserved for Dad. After all his work was physical and he needed the protein.

When we heard that Jessie Fiddes' cow was soon to calve we knew we were in for a special treat indeed. We looked forward to the delicious 'beestings',[12] pudding. This thick, curdled yellow liquid, looked disgusting in the basin, like vomit, but when baked as a pudding it was the most delectable flavor ever to pass my lips. For a couple of days before the cow's mature milk began to flow Jesse gave my family a quantity of the surplus beestings. Mum baked a savoury pudding while Jesse created a kind of egg custard dessert for her family. Mum's was delicious but Jessie's was heavenly.

My mother had little time to bake puddings or cakes. To make up for it, as a special treat before bedtime, she would sometimes indulge us with 'boilie'. She broke stale bread into pieces and shared these between our bowls. We counted our bits to make sure we had not been cheated. She poured boiling milk over the bread and sprinkled it with sugar. We left our bowls to cool just long enough for a skin to form on the milk. By now the bread had turned soft, almost like a bread and butter pudding without the egg, sweet, tasty and hot. Perfect to send us off to sleep.

To me my mother was a saint. Imagine my sorrow when I first became aware she had flaws. Saintly chips began to shed

---

12 Beestings was the colloquial name for 'colostrum'; the cow's 'first milk' and a rich source of protein, enzymes and antibodies, essential to the newborn calf. The received wisdom of the day said children would realise those same benefits. Before vaccines and antibiotics beestings was reputed to be a preventative therapy.

exposing a harsher layer beneath the soft surface. She rarely smacked us and when she did we knew we deserved it, but the time she uncharacteristically locked me in the cupboard was unforgivable. She had endured my naughtiness and backchat until her patience exploded. She grabbed me by the arm and pushed me inside the broom cupboard and closed the door tight. Not a chink of light could be seen. I cried loudly to begin with and tried desperately to open the door from the inside but it stuck fast. I quaked with fright as I imagined spiders and other demons creeping towards me from every corner. My cries turned to feeble whimpers and I begged to be let out. "I promise I'll be good now." Mum told me afterwards I had been locked in for just a few seconds but I didn't believe her. She knew I hated the dark – putting me in that blackest of black space was psychological cruelty; hardly saintly. She only needed to threaten me with the cupboard in the future and I behaved.

During my early teenage years I noticed the chips become larger flakes. I was old enough then to understand my mother was human like us all and had just as many faults. This realisation helped me sympathise with my father more. He was fully aware and aggrieved, jealous even, that his children idolised their mother whilst being afraid of their father. He had to compete for her love and attention. Sometimes, at the day's end there was little left for him.

My parents were brought up to 'know their place' and accept their position in society's hierarchy. Yet, Dad had ambition and intelligence, despite his humble background and job. He could have done well in a different life where he might have had more choice. He knew this and throughout his life harboured an underlying frustration and resentment at the barriers that prevented him from greater fulfillment.

An example of this acceptance happened one Sunday in spring when I was nine and John ten. We were playing on the Cement. The day was clear and still, which meant the sudden noise of a crash at the road end half-a-mile away carried clearly to our ears, causing us both to look up. The incident was too far to make out what had happened but we could see two parked cars and people on the road talking. Many minutes passed and nothing happened; we lost interest and carried on with our game. Every now and again we checked to see if anything had changed. People flitted backward and forward between the cars and kept peering into the ditch. One car drove away and returned a while later. Time is difficult to gauge as a child but to us the commotion seemed to last for hours. John suddenly said, "Eee look. There's an ambulance coming doon the road." Its blue light flashed and its bell rang. Our lack of interest quickly changed to mounting curiosity.

"What if someone's dead," John said. His eyes shone with the morbid thought.

We wanted to share the news but the farm seemed deserted. Mum and Dad were out on the motorbike, the Fiddeses were indoors having lunch and the Collinses were nowhere to be found either.

"It's coming doon our road, John." I followed the ambulance's progress as it drove around the dangerous corner and on out of sight as it passed the burn. We gazed toward the farmyard, curious to know if the ambulance would come our way. Maybe it would carry on past the

Thompsons and up the road to Hetton Law; maybe it would go all the way to the hospital at Berwick. What if someone really was dead? The blue light had stopped flashing.

We heard the engine chug, louder now. "It's coming here. I wonder who's in it," John said.

The ambulance drove straight up the slope and came to a halt on the Cement just outside our house. John and I stood motionless and just a little scared. By now the neighbours materialised from their cottages, clearly concerned.

The ambulance doors opened. Mum and Dad emerged, shaken and badly bruised, but alive.

Dad had persuaded Mum to ride pillion on his new BSA motorbike. He knew she was a nervous passenger and said, "Come on Sadie, I won't take yer far. Just up to the school and back." He put on his great coat, his goggles and leather cap with flaps covering his ears and took his position at the front; she sat astride behind him. She wore a green overcoat that flared out from a fitted waist but wore nothing on her head, not even a headscarf. Dad kicked the starting pedal twice before the engine fired.

"Are yer ready Sadie?" he asked with a mischievous grin and a hint of bravado in his voice. Mum responded with a tentative but courageous smile.

On their way back from the school, Dad gradually applied the brakes, slowing the machine to turn at the road end. He could see a car in his wing mirror driving up behind. He paid no attention until it began to overtake. He realised the car was perilously close and tried hard to control the bike. Mum clung to his waist fully aware of the impending danger. The car driver seemed oblivious to the couple and

made no attempt to move out. In fact it moved closer still and forced Mum and Dad off the road.

They tumbled sideways into the ditch and the motorbike fell on top of them. If their speed had been faster their injuries could have been much worse, especially as neither of them wore proper helmets. They each suffered cuts and bruises the size of dinner plates, from hip to ankle on both legs. They fashioned crutches out of upturned brooms and hobbled about the house for a week.

The police persuaded Dad to take the blame for the accident and to not pursue a claim. The lady who had forced them off the road was a magistrate, a justice of the peace. "It'll be better that way, less trouble," the policeman said.

Mum and Dad 'knew their place'.

It was the mid 1950s. The National Health Service was well established. Rationing had come to an end and everyone began to feel the heavy weight of austerity lift. Wage packets increased and even my parents enjoyed a slightly better living standard. Money was still tight but they could now afford an additional tin of tobacco and cigarette papers to cater for an extra smoker. Dad, who had been smoking for years, encouraged Mum to join him. Before long a smoke fug filled our tiny living room polluting the ceiling and walls; they turned yellow from nicotine stain. Paddy, Hubert and Kathleen were teenagers at this time and inquisitive about the habit that had gripped our parents. They didn't have the nerve to pinch the real tobacco and instead, tried to make their own. They took sheets of hard Izal toilet paper, see-through, like tracing paper and put strips of tealeaves down the centre. They licked the edges and rolled them into shape. Their ingenuity had to be applauded even though their homemade cigarettes would never burn.

The National Health brought with it cod liver oil. Once a week Mum made us swallow a dose. We invented many creative reasons why we should not be taking it. She would listen and simply say, "Well you don't say. Is that right. Now, open yer mouth." The spoonful of sugar that followed did little to disperse the most disgusting taste ever to pass down my throat.[13] Syrup of figs followed, which we probably didn't need. All her adult life my mother had difficulty "going to the toilet", her delicate description for her condition. She determined her children would not suffer the same. Rose-hip syrup provided us with all our vitamin C needs; this sweet red liquid we didn't mind at all.

Dental care became more accessible under the NHS and my parents took advantage of it. I recall walking into the

---

13 I have never liked fish since.

living room one day to see my dad sitting in his armchair by the fire. He held a hot-water bottle wrapped in a towel against his cheeks, which were swollen to twice their size. He glowered with bad temper and looked thoroughly wretched. His mouth had disappeared beneath the puffy bulge. When he tried to talk the words dribbled in a bloody slur.

Mum told me he had been to the dentist in Berwick and had all his teeth removed, that I shouldn't bother him because he was in great pain.

"What for," I asked, astonished anyone would do such a thing.

"Because some of his teeth were going bad and giving him the toothache," she replied.

"But why did he have to have them all out?" I couldn't understand why the dentist didn't just remove the bad ones.

"The dentist said he should, before the others went bad as well."

The idea of such advice seemed bizarre to me. I learned later this was common practice in the 1950s. Many of the adult population suffered tooth decay and, for those who were unable to afford more expensive treatment, the dentistry wisdom at the time was to just get rid of the lot of them. It would be cheaper in the long run.[14]

After the swelling receded Dad's bad-tempered surfaced all over again as he struggled to get used to his new dentures.

My parents remained together for the rest of their lives. It was a less than perfect marriage and there were many upsets and disagreements, particularly with regard to Dad's harsh

---

14 Thank goodness for water fluoridation and modern dentistry techniques.

punishments. But perhaps their personality differences enabled them to maintain some kind of equilibrium. My mother did consider leaving Dad at one stage and asked me what I thought about it. I was thirteen. My own relationship with him at the time was troubled but I burst into tears none-the-less, worried about how he could possibly cope by himself.

My parents made me who I am. The responsibility of providing for a large family on their dismal wages, particularly in the early years, must have been burdensome and a great worry at times. They survived, and pulled us all through instilling their moral code along the way.

# Chapter 14

# Entrances and Exits

I watched my mother grow fat. She was 36 years old and from being slim all her life she now hauled her heavy body across the room and struggled to ease herself into and out of the armchair. Not until she was at least seven months pregnant did someone explain to me that she was expecting a baby. Until then I failed to understand why her belly swelled and why she tolerated me less. Certainly the information didn't come from her; my mother preferred to divert such questions. She even forced my sister Kathleen to tell me about the 'birds and bees'. On a quiet afternoon, when the men were in the fields and the women were indoors chatting over a cup of tea, I found myself sitting on the Cement with my brother John and June Fiddes. Kathleen sat between us and described exactly how babies were created. I reacted the same way all children do, shock that my parents could do such a thing, and already six times. Now they had done 'it' a seventh time. Not only that, after eight years my position as the youngest family member was to be usurped.

Previously Mum had been giving birth every eighteen months. Birth control was strictly against Catholic doctrine therefore an eight-year gap seemed strange. Perhaps, once out of sight of the beady eyes of the priest in Malin Head, my parents used some form of protection and were willing to risk the 'wrath of God'. But no protection is fool-proof.

In September 1958 an ambulance arrived and took Mum to the hospital in Gosforth, Newcastle, sixty miles south. Complications with the pregnancy meant she had to have an emergency Caesarian. My baby sister Sally entered into the family six weeks early. She was christened Sarah (like Mum), Patricia but would always be called Sally. Newcastle was too far for Dad to visit. It must have been difficult for my mother, miles from home without loved ones to provide comfort. During that time Kathleen took care of us – Dad, four brothers and me. She was only fourteen but handled the responsibility like a grown up. She cooked, cleaned, washed clothes and ensured John and I got to school on time. At eight years old, I was confused by these changes and pined for my mother.

She came home two weeks after the birth. Her stitches had healed enough to enable her to be discharged. She should have taken it easy in recovery but felt guilty that Kathleen had already missed too much school. Her Catholic upbringing demanded she accept the guilt and bear the consequences. She got out of bed the next day, sent Kathleen to school and set about the daily chores. I was overjoyed that my mother was home. Life would get back to normal, or so I thought. Her attention was directed, not at me, but at this tiny creature asleep in her crib. I became aware of a new emotion I could not ignore - jealousy.

How life had changed for my parents. After eight years free of newborns they were thrust once more into screeching cries in the night and disrupted sleep. As the months passed Sally grew into a bonny baby with large hazel eyes and a bunch of curls. My dad became smitten and for the first time spoiled his child. Sally developed eczema a year later and was tormented by terrible itching. She scratched until her skin split and bled. My mother would tie a pair of old socks over her hands to stop her from damaging herself further. To compound this Sally also developed asthma and other allergies. The poor little mite suffered wheezing bouts and allergic reactions that, in years to come, would see her in hospital more than once, close to anaphylactic shock. My dad couldn't bear to see his little darling suffer this way and spoiled her all the more.

It took time for me to become used to my new sister. I resented Dad's orders to give up my play and soothe Sally's itches until she slept. I must have crept away a hundred times thinking she was asleep only to rush back at her whines and renew my stroking. As a three year old she was persistent in her demands for the use of my pencils and ruler just when I was trying to complete my homework. Dad forced me to give them up to her, fuelling my growing resentment. It wasn't her fault - she had been used to having her own way.[15]

Yet there were times we did have fun with our baby sister. John and I would push her up and down the Cement in her black pram with wheels the size of a cart's. When Mum wasn't looking we would let the pram go at the top of the slope and watch it roll into the farmyard, gathering speed as it went. We ran after it and caught it at the bottom. Sally's baby giggles were so funny we did it again and again.

The pram tipped over once and she bounced into the grass verge, where she lay motionless long enough for us to think we had killed her. When the shock subsided her giggles were louder than ever. We were lucky and continued with the game, undeterred.

---

15 As we grew into adulthood I began to forgive her

Kathleen was the first to exit the household. She turned fifteen in November the year Sally was born and left school at Christmas. My parents found her a job in a hotel in Hawick, a mill town in the Scottish Borders. The sooner she went out to work the sooner she could send money home. Mum bought her a blue and yellow matching coat and dress to help her feel all grown up.

Kathleen's emotions were a mixture of excitement and fear. Excited by this new freedom, but afraid about how she would cope, alone, away from her family and sheltered life. She worked as a chambermaid and waitress. She boarded in the hotel and at first enjoyed the job but before long the maître d' began to ill-treat her. She forced Kathleen to hand over her tips and gave her unpleasant tasks not listed in the job specification, like cleaning dirty staff toilets. Kathleen sent a portion of her wage packet home and, with her tips in the hands of her tormentor, found she was short of money. This curtailed her freedom to explore the town and the entertainment it had to offer. She began to hate the job and stayed in her room, which she regarded as a prison cell. After three months she decided she'd had enough and came home at Easter, refusing to go back. Instead she found herself a seasonal job in a guesthouse in Holy Island, which she loved.

During this time she met her first boyfriend, Jackie Potts and brought him home one weekend to meet the family. I looked up at this handsome young man with dark sleeked back hair and at once became love-struck. He talked to me, teased and tickled me and generally tolerated me. I yearned for their weekend visits. When the romance came to an end two years later I wept. Mum said to me, "Sure there'll be time enough for boyfriends when you get older." She and Kathleen smiled conspiratorially when they thought I wasn't looking.

At the season's end Kathleen found work in Berwick. For the next three years she did various mundane jobs; she worked with children, in a laundry, and in a bakery. She knew she was capable of much more so enrolled in night school to learn shorthand, typing and bookkeeping. Her childhood dream had been to become a nurse and at the age of eighteen she was accepted as an auxiliary in Berwick Infirmary. The matron could see that Kathleen had ability and encouraged her to take the State Enrolled Nursing entrance exam. She passed the exam and moved to Hexham soon after to begin her training. She came home at weekends as often as she could with many stories to tell. I listened from my bed to Mum's howls of laughter coming from the living room and longed to be with them to listen too. I was told to stay in bed and go to sleep.

Kathleen qualified as an SEN two years later. She went on to gain her State Registered Nursing qualification and later still became a Sister.

In 1959 Hubert was the next to leave. He had finished school a year earlier than Kathleen, also at the age of fifteen, and had worked on the farm until his application to join the Royal Naval Cadets was accepted. He couldn't wait to leave the claustrophobia of Hetton Hall, and Dad's authoritarianism. At the age of 16 he walked to the road end to catch the bus to Berwick, the first leg of a long trip to HMS Ganges in Shotley, Suffolk, as far from home as possible. He never looked back. After completing his cadet training Hubert graduated as an aircraft engineer. He joined the Fleet Air Arm on the aircraft carrier HMS Ark Royal. His narrow existence in Hetton Hall now expanded to include the world's oceans and ports. His athleticism and sheer determination gained him a place on the Fleet Air Arm's gun crew. In the early 1960s his team took part in the Royal Tournament military tattoo contest at Earls Court Exhibition Centre. The contest's aim was to carry a twelve-pound field gun over a series of challenging obstacles, to cross the 'enemy' wall and return the way they had come. Not only did his team win that year but they also set a world record.

One night, approximately a year after he joined HMS Ark Royal, Mum woke to a disturbance. The sound came from Joe and John's bedroom. She got up wondering what the matter was with the boys. Normally they slept so soundly. She often said to them, "Yous two could be murdered in your beds and not know it." She crept out into the corridor and was confronted by a tall, dark shape blocking her path. Panicked she cried, "Jesus, Mary and Joseph," and was about to shout for help when the intruder said, "Don't be scared Mum. It's only me." Hubert emerged from the darkness. He had been given unexpected leave and decided to come home - but he had no way to inform our parents. He arrived in Berwick late at night and, with no other means of transport, walked the ten miles to Hetton Hall. In the early hours he dropped his kit bag outside Joe and John's bedroom window, pulled up the sash and manoeuvred his body through the narrow gap. The boys remained in a deep sleep. Mum hugged him hard, delighted to have her son home and said, "Sure, you'll be dying for a cup of tea."

How handsome my older brother looked in his naval uniform. I would try on his white cap and flick the blue flap that fell around his shoulders; and why oh why did those voluminous trousers have rows and rows of horizontal creases? Tall and dark, Hugh had grown. No longer the boy that recoiled from his father's raised hand but a man who stood inches above him. Dad would think twice now before inflicting physical punishment, justified or not.

The next to depart was Joe. His unhappy start in our family kept him on the edge and slightly isolated. He and Dad never settled their differences. I can remember arguments between the two where, on more than one occasion, I heard Dad shout, "Get out of this house and don't ever come back." Joe would storm out and return later when both had calmed down. Mum did her best to broker reconciliation, determined not to lose her son a second time.

Joe resolved not to become locked in farm work drudgery and decided to follow in Hubert's footsteps and sail the oceans. His final school report was cruel and unforgivable – to be told that if he ever had any brains he lost them a long time ago did nothing for his confidence. Joe was certain the Royal Navy would turn him down. Rather than be humiliated with rejection he joined the less prestigious Merchant Navy as an Ordinary Seaman.[16]

The captain of one of the ships that Joe served on saw his potential. He took it upon himself to mentor Joe. He taught him maths and other subjects until he felt Joe was ready to try for the first of his officer tickets. With this special attention and encouragement Joe completed the training and passed the exam in half the time. Over the next few years he progressed to become First Mate.

On trips home he always brought me a present; my favourite, a blue-netted petticoat. He and I formed a lasting bond without realising it – at least I didn't at the time.

When Joe left the Merchant Navy to join Trinity House he gained his Master's ticket. Quite an achievement for someone who had no brains.

Paddy, my eldest brother stayed at home. After leaving school he took on a motor mechanic apprenticeship at a garage in Holborn, three miles from Hetton Hall. He and Dad were on better terms. Both enjoyed dabbling with engines. Dad's head would be under the bonnet of our green Ford Poplar while Paddy's would be examining his BSA

---

16 The irony is that Joe was clever and astute and in later life prospered – more than any of us. He just hated school and academia.

motorbike engine. After a year or so into his apprenticeship his flair with engines became well known. His friends and acquaintances sought his skills; even Father Devlin brought his car to Paddy for repair. Many a weekend the Cement outside our house was littered with motorbike parts. Paddy's pals would hang around waiting for the repairs, and while he tinkered Mum brewed tea for the young men, until each motorbike roared into life once more.

Paddy came home each night covered in grease from a day at work underneath engines. Mum helped him pick out black wax from his ears and he spent ages in the scullery scrubbing the oil stains from his skin and nails.

He was the constant older brother; always home in the evening. He possessed a mean streak, just like Dad. He drank his tea black and liked to cool it down with cold water. He would order John or I to fetch it and if we refused he would clip us around the head until we did as we were told. I don't remember him ever playing with us, but then why would he? He was ten years older.

Paddy liked to appear hard. His innocent face and fair hair belied his nature. Always up for a fight he joined the school boxing team and would fight in matches across the county. One harsh winter, when snow had been falling in blustery storms for days, the farm finally became cut off in white isolation. The weekly food vans were unable to get through and eventually our basic food stocks ran low. Folks in the other cottages struggled in the same way. It became clear the snow was set to continue for days. Something had to be done about the food supply. A group of men, one from each cottage, decided to brave the walk to Lowick for provisions. Paddy volunteered from our cottage.

My mother pleaded with him, "What sort of a notion is that? Yer'll do no such thing. It's too far in this weather. Yer far too young." Paddy was seventeen and determined to endure the journey. After all, he was hard. I watched Mum fuss over him, her face creased with anxiety. She found him jumpers, coats, scarves and woolly hats and helped him wrap up warm. Paddy set out with his companions, not yet a man, but courageous and stubborn. Mum stood by the window, her eyes intent on her firstborn as he clambered down the slope to the farmyard. One leg, then the other disappeared into the drifts leaving behind deep holes where his feet had trodden. No sooner had Paddy turned the corner, out of sight, than it started to snow heavily again. The foot-holes quickly vanished.

It took the party many hours to trudge the six miles to Lowick and six miles back. They followed the lanes as best they could where the snow lay less thick. At last they returned with as much provision as they could carry. Paddy was hard, but the quest had taxed him; the cold, the tiredness, twelve miles of tramping, had sapped his strength. His cocky tenacity took quite a knock that day. Paradoxically, his lack of strength during this ordeal made him more a man. [17]

Then everything changed. Kathleen had been home the weekend of February 20th 1961. Joy Lamb, Paddy's girlfriend was also visiting. That night John and I shared a bed because Joy was staying the night and would use my room. We were woken in the early hours by loud wails

17 Why my father didn't go instead of Paddy, I do not know

coming from the living room. I heard Joy Lamb's voice shout, "Paddy, Paddy!" Her lament caused a twinge of fear to creep into the pit of my stomach. Moments later the bedroom door opened, the light switched on, Mum and Dad walked over. By now, John and I knelt on top of the covers knowing something terrible had happened.

The human brain tries to trick us when we want to believe something other than reality. For a split second, as Mum and Dad walked over to the bed, I believed all was fine; there had been no tragedy. But then reality cruelly tosses the trick aside. Mum sat on the bed and put her arms around us, her face wretched, I could smell her grief. Amid heaving sobs she whispered, "Paddy is dead." A thunderbolt struck. It shook me to the core and I howled Joy's same words, "Paddy, Paddy!"

We wept and wept. My Mum cradled us, and Dad stood above with his arm stretched along the back of the iron frame headboard. Tears clouded his eyes. To see my dad cry was almost as shocking. Dads did not cry.

I reacted with an odd fierceness, which was strange. I didn't like Paddy much. He was mean and insisted I fetch cold water for his tea; other than that he paid me little attention. But he was my brother and perhaps sibling bonds run deep, even in a ten year old.

Kathleen blamed herself. She had wanted to stay at home as long as possible and asked Paddy if he would give her a lift on his motorbike to her Berwick lodgings in the evening.

"I'll have to catch the bus if you don't. I don't want to leave that early."

"No," he said. "Sorry, but the lights on the bike aren't working properly."

"Please. Can't you fix the lights?"

Reluctantly he agreed and put in a temporary repair.

If only she had caught the bus. The repair lasted the journey to Kathleen's digs but on the way back the motorbike lights failed again. Paddy parked the bike on the side of the A1 to fix them. The night was black and he wore dark leathers. As he knelt on the ground a passing car struck him. It dragged him for two hundred yards, breaking his body in the process. The driver had been drunk but he had the presence of mind to find help.

Mum and Dad sat by Paddy's hospital bed. Mum prayed and prayed to God her first son might live, but he never regained consciousness and died from internal injuries at 2:00 a.m. My mother lost a part of her faith that night.

Hubert came home on compassionate leave several days afterwards. I remember his arrival so well. John and I were asked to go out because the house was full of people offering their condolences. Hubert walked up the slope. He looked dashing in his sailor's uniform. Mum greeted him on the doorstep. He dropped his kitbag on the Cement, I can still hear the thud, and gave her a long, long hug.

Paddy's grave was beautiful. Many sympathisers sent wreaths, which completely covered the grave and beyond.

He had been a motorbike enthusiast and took part in local trials and triumphed many times. After successfully completing his apprenticeship a month before, he had found a job as a mechanic to a motorbike racing team in Snetterton, Suffolk and had been planning to leave home the following month.

Instead, at only twenty years old Paddy's exit from the family was a cruel tragedy.

My parents immersed themselves in a kind of stunned sadness. Mum couldn't bear to live in Hetton Hall any longer. The memories were too painful. Dad looked for work and was offered two separate steward jobs on other farms, both a promotion. One position was further south and one at West Kyloe, six miles north-east of Hetton Hall and closer to the coast. Mum preferred to move to West Kyloe – the distant sea view reminded her of her 'real' home in Malin Head.

In May that year we moved from Hetton Hall a much smaller family but by then Mum was pregnant again. In the coming September yet another new baby would enter the family.

# Chapter 15

# West Kyloe

My mother's pregnancy helped her look forward to the future. The involuntary, heavy dry sobs, which had peppered her day, lessened with each little kick from her unborn child, reminding her she was still a mother. I yearned for her to be happy again, to sing the old Irish songs again, and to be my mum again – whole. Moving to West Kyloe added to the healing process and as her belly grew, so her old self emerged, until one day she threw back her head, clasped her hands to her chest, opened her mouth wide and laughed out loud, just like she used to. She had come back to me at last.

West Kyloe was a privately owned farm a mile west of the A1, the Great North Road. The house we moved into was a stone built, two-storey end of terrace in a row of four, situated on a rise above the farm. We occupied the house at the north end of the terrace. It had once been two cottages that had been knocked into one. It had two large reception rooms as well as a kitchen, a downstairs loo and a bathroom upstairs. Mum, Dad, John, Sally, me and my cat Tiger all crossed the threshold into more space than we ever dreamed of. What luxury, no more waiting outside the toilet with crossed legs.

"If only we'd had this to live in when we were all at home," Mum said.

The distant Farne Islands could be seen from the house. Mum would stand at the window and gaze at the sea view. "Sure it reminds me of home."

My father settled into his steward's role and enjoyed the small amount of power he wielded over the farm labourers, as well as the extra money he earned. As in Hetton Hall I saw little of him.

Mr Hogg, the farmer, lived in the big house beyond the copse, which led down to the farm buildings, out of sight of our terrace. He was an elusive boss but we sometimes spotted him walking the lanes carrying a walking stick, always wearing a tweed jacket, plus fours and thick socks that came up to his knees. Dad often scoffed at his clothes saying, "He's a right posh bastard."

Our neighbours made us feel welcome and at home. The day we arrived, Sam and Mary Dunne, who lived at the other end of the terrace, came to say hello, brewed us tea and offered to help in any way. They were a delightful and enlightened couple in their fifties. They stood the same height, squat and slightly dumpy, and could have been twins. They had two grown up daughters, Lillian and Marion. Lillian had married and lived further afield. Marion taught PE at a senior school in Berwick and lived with her parents. I liked her a lot. She talked to me as an adult and told me tales of her exotic trips to Oslo and other parts of the world. A tall, slender lady called Betty, who taught at the same school, lodged with them. She and Marion were close friends. [18]

---

18 How close I didn't learn until much later. At the time the subject of their relationship wasn't talked about.

Sam and Mary adored Sally and would take her into their house for whole days and spoil her as much as Dad did. Directly next door to them lived Old Mrs Bryson and her son Geordie. He was five foot six inches tall, shorter than my dad - dark haired and in his forties. He worked on the farm and never married. He kept chickens and when he and Dad went to the pub in Lowick on a Saturday night, he would ask John and me to put the chickens to bed at dusk.

"Now make sure they all run up the ramp and dinne' forget to lock the hutch. Otherwise the oul' fox will get em."

We didn't mind this chore one bit because Geordie always brought us each a Cadbury's Dairy Milk chocolate bar. We were less keen on the large bottles of fizzy orange he sometimes brought but didn't dare tell him for fear of getting nothing at all in the future.

The house directly next door to ours was occupied by a succession of families who came and went, never staying long enough to develop a friendship.

A week after we moved to West Kyloe, John and I walked twenty yards from our lane to the Lowick road and waited for the school bus, which would take us to our new schools in Belford, a village on the A1 five miles south. John was joining the secondary modern while I attended the neighbouring junior school. I felt nervous but looked forward to the novelty of riding on a bus. John on the other hand fidgeted and pulled at his new school uniform, unhappy he was being forced to wear a tie.

"I cannut see why you don't you have to wear a blinkin' uniform," he grumbled.

The bus arrived and we climbed aboard and walked towards the back until we found a seat together amid stares and mutterings. We were the new kids and could hear whispers all the way to Belford.

My school was a long, narrow, mostly single-storey building with small windows stretching its length. It used to be the primary, junior and secondary all in one. When pupil numbers outgrew its capacity a new, shiny secondary modern was built across from the playing field in 1959, the year before we moved to West Kyloe.

Compared to Hazelrigg this school was vast. I felt I would get lost among the many classrooms. My class teacher, a middle-aged lady, had a statuesque figure and wore thin, gold-rimmed spectacles. When she removed them they dangled from a chain around her neck. She helped me settle in. I think she liked me because I showed promise. [19]

John and I embraced our new home with excitement and curiosity. Different places to explore – woods, gorse fields, hills and crags and a pond, which, in springtime teemed with frog spawn. We were the only young children on the farm, which was unusual. It meant we relied on each other all the more for amusement. Keeping ourselves occupied was sometimes a challenge that summer. We climbed the hay bales in the hay barn despite severe warnings not to and jumped from the top to a loose hay mound on the ground. One time a pitchfork had been carelessly buried in the hay. John leapt and landed on the handle causing the fork to flip up. The prongs missed his face by an inch. That day

---

19 I wish I could remember her name.

we learned the dangers of such reckless games and why we were forbidden from playing in the barn. We carried on all the same but not before checking the loose hay carefully for hidden objects. We were never caught.

At other times we rode rusty old bicycles without tyres, from the top of the gorse field to the bottom by the pond. We weaved in and out of gorse bushes to see who could reach the bottom first without getting scratched. Up we pushed and down we rode, again and again. It seemed a crazy activity but the long summer holiday inspired creative thinking.

When bored with each other's company, we sometimes cycled to Hetton Hall to play with June and John Fiddes. Our bikes were rickety old machines without lights, but by then, they did have tyres. It took at least an hour to ride those six and a half hilly miles.

"I wish we had gears," I whined, when we were forced, at each steep stretch, to get off the bikes and push. We often forgot the time while playing with the Fiddeses and ended up having to cycle the last part of the journey home in darkness.

Part of that route bordered the Kyloe Forest, which, in the twilight, always caused me a great deal of anxiety. Thick, tall conifers cast deep shadows. It seemed to me the road past the forest stretched for miles, whereas, in truth it was approximately a mile. John could cycle faster and would leave me behind, shouting, "Scaredy cat, scaredy cat."

I hated him just then and no matter how hard I pedalled, his outline moved further and further from view.

I knew he was afraid too but he would never admit it. I was alone and tried to ignore the whispers that emanated from within the forest.

On September 9th 1961 my brother Michael was born. In some ways Mum took solace that he was a boy; not that he was a replacement for Paddy, more that he filled a male space. This bundle of softness and vulnerability was a novelty to me and I experienced none of the jealousy I felt when Sally was born. The little man also developed eczema and asthma when he reached a year old, just as Sally had done at that age. However he received none of the love and special treatment Dad had showered on her. Throughout his young life Michael suffered the same punishments and humiliations Dad had dished out to us older siblings – and especially to his sons.

When Michael turned eighteen months old and Sally four, Hubert announced he was marrying a girl called Mary, from Somerset. Hubert was stationed in Yeovilton at the time and the wedding was to be held in Stoke-sub-Hamdon, a small village not far from Yeovil. It could hardly have been further away from home. Dad refused to attend the wedding; his and Hubert's relationship had remained distant over the years. Mum on the other hand yearned to go. After all Hubert would be the first of her brood to wed. How could she though? Who would look after us younger children while Dad was at work? She resigned herself to staying at home.

When Sam and Mary learned of her dilemma they kindly offered to keep a watchful eye over us and prepare our meals. At first Mum protested; she couldn't possibly expect them to be responsible for her little ones. Gradually, over a period of days, the couple persuaded her we would be fine. Mum finally agreed and began to look forward to her son's wedding.

Kathleen was to be a bridesmaid and had arranged for her boyfriend to drive both her and Mum to Somerset in his mini. They were to be away for five days. Mum had never been a good traveller therefore the long journey in a mini, not known for comfort, would have been an endurance test she would have struggled with.[20]

Sam and Mary were wonderful. Mary brought us meals, although I remember having to do some of the cooking. Sam told us silly jokes that made us laugh. He was always around when we needed him. Sally spent most of her time at their house and came home at bedtime. This helped relieve some of the parenting duties John and I were expected to take on. I adored Michael and played with him often but taking care of him and doing housework was quite enough to deal with

---

20 Many years later Mac and I took her on a long journey, also to the West Country to see Hubert and also in a mini. She was sick on that trip too.

at the age of twelve. I had helped Mum change Michael's terry nappies in the past and learned how to fold and pin them; now I was also forced to wash the stinking baby poo from them. I held my nose tight or stopped breathing until the job was done, and then hung them on the line. Michael, a typical toddler, had an inquisitive mind; keen to investigate everything he came across. John and I chased him, chastised him, and cuddled him when he cried, but the heavy weight of responsibility burdened us both. Sam and Mary were never far away and Dad always came home for lunch, though when Dad came in from work in the evenings he expected us to wait on him with cups of tea, or lay out his dinner. He did nothing to help with Michael, not even tuck him in bed.

When I heard the purr of the mini, which brought my mother home, I too purred - with relief.

A few weeks into the autumn term of 1961 I sat my 11+ and I remember thinking the questions were relatively easy. At the end of the exam I felt confident I'd answered most of them. Then I forgot all about it.

Six months later, four pupils: myself, Douglas, Marion and David, were summoned to the headmaster's office. We each looked at one another wondering if we were in trouble. Our classmates looked on as we left the room and wondered the same. We climbed the stairs to the office with mounting anxiety and knocked on the headmaster's door.

"Two of you have passed your 11+ and will go to the grammar school in Berwick. But I'm afraid two of you have 'just failed'." Those were the headmaster's words as we stood before him.

After school I cried in my mother's arms at my disappointment; I had felt sure I would pass. The headmaster had emphasised the 'just failed' but it did not make me feel any better. I was a failure. In September, Douglas and Marion would go to the grammar school and I would join my brother at the secondary modern across the field.[21] No longer did I ooze confidence or run around talking the 'hind legs off a donkey,' as my mother used to say. Instead, part of me became quiet and insecure.

I joined the secondary modern in September 1962 and settled in to lessons that weren't grammar school lessons. None-the-less I was put in the top stream and thrived. Before long my form teacher, Miss Robertson, recommended I join the second year group for English and Arithmetic. I performed well. As a result the headmaster put me forward for the 12+ exam. A teacher drove me to Alnwick to take the test. I found myself in a large hall full of other candidates, none of whom I knew. I felt alone and afraid. The scrape of chairs being pulled under desks as each entrant took their seat echoed around the chamber and grated on my already tingling nerves. The exam was difficult and I failed. The following year I returned to that same hall and took the 13+ exam. I failed that too. I would have benefited from extra coaching for these exams because the secondary modern curriculum was woefully inadequate for the tests. Had I known this, my humiliation

21 I later learned the qualification rate for 11+ varied considerably around the country. If I had lived in an area where there had been more grammar schools, in the bigger cities for instance, I would probably have passed. I wasn't to know that then, so failing my 11+ had a profound effect on me, which stayed with me well into adulthood

may not have been so marked. Instead of feeling proud that my teachers thought me bright enough to take the exams, three failures just increased my insecurity.

One morning in early November 1962, John and I heard the clatter of horses' hooves - lots of them. We ran from the house and to our delight, the Hunt trotted from the main road into our lane and assembled at the end of the cottages. The riders looked splendid, some in red and others in black jackets, worn above white jodhpurs. I had never seen such a sight, nor had I ever heard of the Hunt. Who were they and why were they gathering at our farm? The hounds ran backward and forward sniffing among the hedgerows. John and I were desperate to move closer, not least so we could pet the hounds, but our shyness held us back. Mr Hogg, wearing his plus fours, appeared carrying a tray of small glasses and two bottles of liquor. He poured whisky for the men and sherry for the ladies. The riders sipped their tipples and made merry with much laughter. A young woman caught sight of our blonde heads and beckoned us over.

We walked slowly toward her and the rest of the group, red-faced with embarrassment. The hounds picked up our scent and ran to greet us. Within seconds those high-spirited dogs surrounded us with nuzzles and sniffs and almost knocked us over in their enthusiasm. Close up, the horses radiated magnificence. I had been used to ponies at Hetton Hall but these animals were in a different league. I longed to stroke their coats that gleamed in the pale November light. The Master sensed my yearning and said, "Would you like to come up and sit in the saddle?"

Oh my, how grand and important I felt. High off the ground I was as proud as I had ever been. Alas, the moment was fleeting. The Hunt must make chase. The Huntsman sounded his horn; the hounds lifted their heads and collected into a pack in front of the horses, baying in anticipation. Then they were off. Horses and hounds cantered down the lane throwing up dust clouds. John and I watched until the last red jacket disappeared and the dust settled once more.

I had no perception of what the Hunt meant, or the torment and terror the fox would be subjected to. Nor had I ever seen the Hunt galloping over fields in chase. The CWS land at Hetton Hall was laid over to arable and livestock so the Hunt would not have been permitted to ride across it.

To me it looked like adventure. I hoped some day I might be lucky enough to take part.[22]

As in Hetton Hall taking a bath in our West Kyloe house was rationed to once a week. My mother thought it unnecessary to bathe more than that. Consequently, when I slipped into the deep hot water I liked to take time. One day, while luxuriating in the heat, growing pinker by the minute, a piece of plaster fell into the bath water. Another followed this and then a large chunk of the ceiling came crashing down around me. I screamed and leapt out of the water, grabbed a towel just as Mum came in to find out what the fuss was about. She glared at the plate-sized hole in the plaster, then at the mess in the bath water and then at me.

---

22 Years later I became fully aware of their activities and the horrific conclusion to their ride. I found myself standing among other protesters 'booing' at the red jackets as they rode by

"Jesus, are you alright? Are you hurt?" I don't know why she asked Jesus, it was me who had the fright. My only injuries were a couple of scratches on my shoulder and a bruised modesty.

At the beginning of the summer term in 1964 excitement buzzed through the corridors at school.

"Are you gannin on the school trip?" Everybody asked each other this question. "No'" said some, disappointed. "Yes," said others, delighted.

I felt certain John and I would not be allowed to go. How could our parents afford to send two children away for five days? When she said, "Aye, you can go," I jumped up and down, thrilled at the prospect and hugged her tight.

She found the money from somewhere and a week after the Whitsun break John and I walked out to the road carrying our packed bags to wait for the school bus. As we climbed aboard I saw Mum come out to the bread van, which had just arrived. I knew she would be feeling tired - she had been up late the night before drying and ironing our clothes. No way would we be the rag-tag children among our schoolmates. I felt a twang of guilt and resolved to help her more on my return.

Anticipation hummed in the school playground as the trippers hung around waiting for the coach. This was a major trip for us rural children, whose horizons were small. The coach driver dropped us at Ford, a village thirteen miles inland from Belford. Twenty-five children gaped in disbelief at the magnificent castle, which stood before us.

"Is that where we are staying miss?" someone asked.

"It is," she replied.

A medieval castle, it commanded a position among rolling hills and stunning scenery in the Northumbrian countryside. It had been built as a defense against the Scots. In 1513 King James IV of Scotland crossed the border and occupied it temporarily while fighting King Henry VIII's forces at the battle of Flodden. We learnt all this during our stay. After a long and diverse history and a number of restorations it was now a residential centre for young people, full of dark recesses and suits of armour.

I had never been away from my parents and wondered if I would be homesick. Not a bit of it. We explored the myriad of corridors and extensive rooms and spent the days taking part in fun outdoor and indoor activities. We split into groups and I spent an afternoon by a stream with Ishbel Baptie and Linda Falla searching for wild flowers and ferns, and anything else of interest. I entertained the two girls with my best Irish accent saying, "Will you the pass the water down?" The only phrase I could come up with that sounded at all Irish. We ate in a grand hall and slept in dormitories.

The week culminated in a group photograph on the entrance steps (I'm in the front row, fourth from the right. John is in the second row, third from the right), followed by a party at which we sang and danced to modern pop tunes. Whenever I listen to 'The Island of Dreams' by the Springfields, I think of Ford castle and that magical week.

Back home Mum said, "Your cousin Kathleen is coming to visit." Kathleen arrived from Malin Head two weeks later. She was six years my senior and had short dark hair and freckles. My memory of her from previous visits to Malin Head was vague. I was surprised to see her limp into the hallway and drag her left foot. I then noticed one of her legs was shorter than the other and that she wore a built-up shoe. The shoe must have been a poor fit because it did little to disguise her lameness. She had contracted polio as a child but was determined to maintain her independence. "Sure look at her," Mum said, "she's a marvel travelling all that way from home to here by herself."

Kathleen was a skilled seamstress and offered to make me a dress. Mum owned an old sewing machine that folded away in a cabinet. The sewing machine rusted away in its slot but the cabinet, draped with a pretty lace runner, served as a piece of furniture in the living room. Kathleen restored and threaded the machine. She proceeded to stitch up a simple cotton shift dress with a tiny orange check. I watched in fascination as she cut out the pattern pieces and was even more intrigued at how the garment pieced together. I loved this dress and felt all grown up when I wore it. Now I could attend my first dance in Lowick village hall and not feel like the 'have-not' child who had nothing to wear.

"Please can I wear stockings with it Mum? All my friends at school wear them. Please!"

"Your Dad will say no."

"But we don't have to tell him," I pleaded.

"You'll need a suspender belt then," Mum said, relenting.

And so we three females conspired. I put on my first suspender belt and stockings, then the shift dress and new shoes, and for the first time sensed the beginnings of young adulthood. I would be fourteen in October.

I joined my friends at the dance and 'twisted and shouted', and 'shook all over' to the Beatles and the Swingin Blue Jeans, all the while hitching up my stockings, which kept drooping because of the ill-fitting suspender belt. After the dance I crept into the house and rushed to my room in the hope Dad would be in the living room asleep. He came out of the bathroom as I ran past and he undoubtedly saw my stocking clad legs. In my mind it was on that day he stopped talking to me. It may have been some other time, it may have been gradual, I can't be sure. It may have been the stockings or it may not. Something elusive happened between us that caused him to reject me around that time. From then on, any communication was through Mum or John. He would say to John, "Tell your sister to do this", or "tell your sister to make a cup of tea."

I was confused and hurt. Mum told me he found it difficult to accept his little girl was becoming a young woman. This was hard for me to understand. Our relationship had been far from close, but we had communicated. I didn't know how to put it right. All I could do was avoid him as much as possible and hope one day soon he would forgive me for growing up.

# Chapter 16

# Goodbye to the North

My relationship with Dad remained cold. I continued to avoid him as much as possible and he continued to communicate with me through John, usually to tell me to fetch him something or other.

A notable exception occurred when one day two policemen arrived at our door. John and I perked up; interested to know why they wanted to speak to Dad. Were they here to whisk him away to prison? We stayed close, all agog. It transpired the police were carrying out routine weapons checks and wanted to inspect Dad's shotgun and licence.

Dad had shot rabbits in Hetton Hall for food, as had all the farm labourers. Hundreds of the animals bobbed about the fields and when meat was in short supply there was always rabbit. The men would hunt at night and shine a light in the rabbits' eyes, the creatures froze and then bang! Hardly fair game. When myxomatosis struck, it put an end to the rabbit shooting and game meat for dinner.

The dust covered gun lay on the table. Out of the blue Dad turned to me and said in his sweetest, loving voice, "Gan an' fetch me a cloth Margaret to wipe off the dust." I felt wounded at his duplicity, pretending to be nice in front of these officers. I fetched the cloth all the same.

As soon as the police left he returned to his frosty treatment as if I was an unwanted headache.

In early spring 1963 I took my first solo trip to Berwick. At twelve and a half I felt perfectly capable. I had been to the town with Mum previously, shopping. She agreed I could go but insisted I return after a couple of hours.

I savoured the sweet taste of freedom as I skipped the mile down the Fenwick road to catch the bus. I took myself into town many times after that and stayed longer each time. The Fenwick road was quiet and cars infrequent; when I heard an engine I longed for the driver to stop and offer me a lift. They often did and I accepted without question; a mile was a long way, especially when late for the bus. In rural areas like ours the threat of abduction or harm to a child was as far from peoples' minds as a doctor refusing to treat someone in pain. In fact the drivers felt obliged to offer lifts. Mum and Dad thought it perfectly right that people stop and help a stranger. That's what the friendly, neighbourly Malin Head folk would do.

My sister Kathleen worked in Berwick and when the cinema was showing South Pacific she suggested John and I might like to see it. She met us off the evening bus. We were so excited. We'd never been to a real cinema. I watched the film, wide-eyed, enthralled with the colours, the dancing and the songs. My favourite was Bali Hai. Then, half an hour before the film ended Kathleen said, "Sorry kids, it's time to go. The last bus home leaves soon." We were crushed with disappointment.[23]

We stepped off the bus into the night. We had forgotten to bring a torch so stayed close together. After walking

---

23 Perhaps it was just as well because, had I seen the end, I would have shed buckets of tears all the way home at the death of handsome Lieutenant Joe Cable

through the lit streets of Fenwick, darkness surrounded us. A crescent moon served only to cast looming shadows from the hedgerows. We were halfway up the hill when, from directly behind the hedge, came a loud and deep throated cough. Terrified, I threw myself at John. He said, "Run!" I ran as fast as I ever had and didn't even see the usually frightening grotesque headstone shapes in the graveyard further ahead. We crashed through the front door and only then did we stop to consider what we had heard. We stood in the porch and laughed and laughed. Mum came to greet us wanting to know what was funny. She laughed too. We had heard that cough many times during the day but the dark night obscured any rational thought. Even sheep developed coughs.

In September that year, Sally started school. "Now be sure to take care of her on that main road, and make sure you take her all the way to the primary school," were my mother's parting words as we walked out to catch the school bus. I felt a strange pride as I settled her into her seat amid curious stares and comments from the older girls, "Ah, she's a canny wee lass."

On her third day the older girls encouraged Sally to sit at the back of the bus with them. She giggled and squealed when the girls tickled and teased. She was clearly enjoying herself. Fine by me, it gave me a break from being her keeper. When we arrived at school everyone piled off the bus as usual. I walked into the school entrance and suddenly remembered Sally. I scanned the mass of uniforms, but couldn't see her. I had lost my sister. I rushed back toward the bus pushing people aside. I could feel the

tears surface and was unsure of what to do next. My fear
turned to horror when I saw her little face appear at the
back window of the bus just as it moved off. She seemed
calm, perhaps a little confused, as if to say, 'Should I still
be on the bus?' I had a vision of Sally being whisked away
to some far-off place never to be seen again. I ran after the
bus, but as fast as my legs could run, the bus moved faster.
Mum would kill me! Then the bus stopped abruptly at
the bottom of the road. Sally clambered down the steps
just as I reached the door. The bus driver gave me a wink
and a reassuring grin, and drove off. Relief replaced panic
but then frustration replaced relief.

"Why didn't you get off the bus with the girls?" I yelled
at her.

"I was waiting for you to come and fetch me," she
yelled back, indignant.

After a week Sally knew the way and took herself
to the primary school and I enjoyed the freedom from
responsibility.

On another day after school we were told the bus home
would be an hour late. To kill time I took Sally into
the sweet shop in Belford. Inside I spied a deep tray
of roasted peanuts - these were new. The nutty smell
sneaked up my nostrils tempting me to buy a portion.
I had money in my pocket that day and was glad of it.
The shopkeeper filled a greaseproof cone full of these
delicious morsels. On the bus home I gave Sally a small
handful. She put a few into her mouth and within less
than ten seconds spat out a revolting saliva ridden mess
of chewed up peanut pieces.

"Ugh. They're making my mouth feel funny," she said. By the time we arrived home her face had turned scarlet and her lips had swollen to twice their size.

"Jesus Mary and Joseph! What's happened to your sister?" Mum glared at me as if it was my fault. Sally was finding it difficult to breathe. Mum rushed to the kitchen and filled a bowl with boiling water. She put in a few camphor oil drops and encouraged Sally to lean over the bowl while she draped a towel over her head so that it covered the entire basin.

"Now breathe," she told Sally.

It took a couple of hours for the reaction to diminish. This was the first indication that Sally had a severe peanut allergy.[24] I dismissed the terrifying images of what might have happened if she had swallowed them. She must have thought me a horrible sister. First I leave her on the bus and then I nearly kill her with peanuts.

In February 1964 Rosemary and Evelyn Collins came to stay for half-term.

I couldn't wait. I hadn't seen my friends for two years. After we moved to West Kyloe I saw less of them. In that period the girls had been lucky enough to acquire free places at the Catholic Boarding School for Girls, in Berwick. Their parents, Big James and Rose, were Irish immigrants like us, and would have been unable to afford the cost of sending their daughters to the school. Neither girl had passed their 11+. However Rose was determined her daughters should

---

24 In later years Sally was taken to hospital more than once close to anaphylactic shock.

receive a better quality education than a secondary modern could deliver and made enquiries at the Catholic school. Rose had a persuasive nature when it suited her and her sister was a nun in America, which might have influenced the headmistress. The girls were accepted. Big James and Rose had moved to Clacton-on-Sea the previous year and had left the girls behind until a place could be secured for them at the Clacton grammar.

I ran out to greet them as they turned into the lane. I was astonished at how much they had changed and barely recognized them. The last time we met they were tomboys but now they had metamorphosed into slender young ladies, oozing confidence. Rosemary was sixteen and Evelyn fifteen.

Rosemary and Evelyn waved as they turned the corner. "Hello Margaret," they called, "how are you." I stopped in my tracks, shocked. They spoke 'posh'. Their broad Northumbrian brogue had disappeared. Rosemary said it had been a matter of survival.

"It's a school full of girls from 'well-to-do families' who talk 'very nicely'," she said. "We either spoke posh or carried on taking a beating."

Their accents might have been upper-class but they hadn't lost their sense of fun and mischief. They told me about the tricks they played on the nuns and how they would sneak out through the dormitory window at night without being discovered. Listening to them was like reading stories from 'Bunty'. I envied their boarding school experience. Like a puppy I followed them around, copied their exotic handwriting and marvelled at their sketching skills; they must have wanted to 'shoo' me away at times. They brushed their long, straight hair into high ponytails.

Rosemary's gleamed red while Evelyn's shone black. Oh, how I wished I could do the same with mine. I had recently pleaded with Mum to cut my hair. I thought I was far too old for a bushy ringlet 'little girl' hairstyle. Mum agreed and cut it to chin length; she pined at the loss as my ringlets fell on the floor, one after the other. "Oh, your beautiful hair," she said, "It's a damned shame." I had hoped to lose the frizz along with the ringlets. Instead the resultant haircut frizzed all the more, like a wire wool bundle.

Rosemary loved Rugby football. She was lucky that their weekend with us coincided with Ireland playing England in the Five Nations Championship. She pleaded with Mum to watch it on our TV, which we now rented. My previous TV experience consisted of the odd cowboy programme sitting on the floor at the Fiddes' house in Hetton Hall. Now I could watch programmes without waiting to be invited.

Both girls sat glued to the set urging Ireland to win. At each Irish 'try' or 'conversion' Rosemary jumped up, threw her fists above her head and hollered, "Yes!" Evelyn's shrieks were more subdued. I found the game unfathomable and desperately tedious. I couldn't understand what they got from it. Mum sat by the fire in the background sipping tea just as uninterested in the game as me. At each "whoop" and "whoa" she smiled and said, "Jesus, yous two are mad."

Ireland triumphed: 18 points to England's 5.

Rosemary and Evelyn left the boarding school at Easter that year and moved south to join their parents in Clacton.

Also that year my dad traded in his old Austin and bought a Mini van.

"I'll be fetching it at the weekend," he told Mum.

John's eyes all but popped through his glasses. "They're the ones you see on the telly. The Beatles have got one." Dad had bought the van version without side windows, hardly the same kudos as the car John was imagining. The Beatles would scarcely have been seen in a van. Nonetheless the Mini was modern, fashionable, a vehicle John and I could brag about.

I sat on the garden wall with John and waited. We each wanted to be the first to spot the new van drive up the Lowick road.

"When is he ever going to get here?" We had been waiting for at least half an hour and I needed the toilet. We heard the thrum of the engine before we saw it and scrambled to stand on the wall, balancing on the uneven stones, all the better to see.

"There it is," John shouted, "its cream." Our eyes followed the small vehicle to the top of the hill before it went out of sight behind the trees. We scampered to the lane just as Dad turned in from the main road and drove to the front door.

The van was the first exciting event to happen in spring 1964. The second was when my parents announced, "We're leaving West Kyloe. We're moving south to join the Collinses to live in Clacton-on-Sea in Essex."

"Isn't that where all those mods and rocker louts are bashing the hell out each other in the streets?" a neighbour asked. "You'll not be wanting to go there."

Dad had no fear of a few hooligans. He said, "There's plenty work on the buildin's and money to be made." He had travelled south to the Collinses a few weeks earlier and spent two weeks at work. He came home with a wad of money. Decision made.

I had mixed emotions. I was sad to leave my friends. Worse, I would have to join a new school. Worst of all I would be forced to leave Tiger behind. On the other hand Clacton was a holiday town by the sea, full of shops I could walk to. I could experience the beach and amusement arcades and mingle with holidaymakers. My life would be richer from the experience. Even the thought of mods and rockers thrilled me. I would be sure to keep a distance, but how dramatic to see and hear crowds of motorbikes and scooters zoom through the streets, revving their engines, as they roared past. Would I become a 'mod' or a 'rocker'? 'Mod', I think. I preferred their dress; a parka was much more stylish than a fringed leather jacket. Mum said the sun shone brighter in the south. She was happy to leave the isolation of the farm and move to a place with more community, more life, and more importantly, more choice.

In May, Mum and Dad packed the Mini van. Inside, tea crates, boxes and suitcases reached to the roof. Outside, the roof rack overflowed. Just when I thought the vehicle was sure to burst, another box would be slotted in, like the comedy act in which passengers continuously piled out of a Mini; only this was the other way around. Most of our furniture had been sold for a pittance but at least the money received would pay for the fuel for the long journey.

While they finished packing I sat on the step outside old Mrs Bryson's house with Tiger in my lap. I stroked his sleek stripes and felt his deep purrs vibrate through my fingers. I had known my beautiful tom all my life. "I can't take you with me Tiger. There's no room see and you'd hate it in the town. Mrs Bryson and Geordie will look after you." He stood up and nuzzled his head into my neck. I swear it was his way of forgiving me.

"Come on Margaret, it's time to go." Mum opened the van door and ushered me in. Sam and Mary, Mrs Bryson and Geordie came out to say goodbye. They waved us on until we had disappeared over the hill down the road to Fenwick.

Mum sat in the front seat with Michael on her lap. Sally sat in a small, improvised single seat in the back just behind the gear stick. John and I were squashed up on a makeshift back seat that lay on top of boxes and cases. Mum spread a rug and cushions across it for padding. Our heads touched the roof. Other drivers on the Great North Road must have wondered, "What on earth…"

Our sturdy little van, our packhorse - a mere 850cc - strained under the weight but it carried its burden without complaint along the A1, mile after mile.

The journey started off as adventure but after many neck-straining hours, just to be able to see through the front window, the travelling became wearisome. Morning turned to afternoon, afternoon to evening, evening to night, and still we hadn't arrived. Perhaps I slept. Dad drove like an automaton – eyes front, foot on the accelerator, foot on the brake, steer the corner, foot on the accelerator, foot on the brake. I had to admire his concentration.

Late into the night, when lights from other traffic had dwindled, we reached the final stretch of our mammoth journey, our little van alone on the road. The signpost pointed to Colchester one way and Cambridge the other. Dad took the Cambridge turn. My mother, usually so mild, lost her temper. Michael was a dead weight on her lap, she hated travel and she ached with fatigue.

"You've taken the turn for Cambridge instead of Colchester," she yelled at him.

"What yer talking about woman. Course I haven't. We're definitely on the road to Colchester." He wouldn't budge. He finally conceded when he saw a large sign for Cambridge, 10 miles, and not a mention of Colchester. He turned the car around. My heart sank through the cushions and rug, through the boxes and suitcases right to the floor. It would be ages yet. I felt sorry for Dad though; he had been behind the wheel for fifteen hours and could be forgiven for making a mistake. Mum, in no mood to forgive, moaned and grumbled at him and told him he should have listened to her. Sally and Michael slept soundly throughout.

We limped into Clacton at 1:30a.m., a ghost town and to me, a tiny bit frightening. I fancied we were the sole survivors of a catastrophic event. Even then our journey wasn't over. Through a hazy torpor Dad had forgotten the directions to the Collins' house in St Osyth Rd. Who could blame him? By now he had been driving for eighteen hours. He stopped in a layby, dropped his head into his hands and cussed under his breath. Mum hissed through her teeth, "Jesus, what yer doing now."

Both my parents were out of their heads with fatigue. We cruised the streets for another half an hour until Dad at last recognized 54 St Osyth Road. At 2:00a.m. Big James and Rose opened their door. I entered this strange house and was struck by the unfamiliar smell. I would share this home with five adults and seven children for the next nine months before we had the means to buy our own home.

When Big James shut out the night it was as if the door to my childhood closed. I said goodbye and without a backward glance, walked down the passageway to a wholly different life.

# Acknowledgements

How lucky I was to have comments and suggestions on every chapter from Writers on the Edge. It was they who encouraged me to keep going. My thanks to them and, in particular, to Jo Jackson for her wonderful support throughout. Thank you also to Mike Rathbone, Lynn Rathbone and Lesley Foster for casting an independent eye over the manuscript. An extra thank you to Lesley Foster for her proof reading skills.

I extend a special thank you to my sisters Kath and Sally, and to my brother John who helped me out with sketchy and unreliable memories.

Lorna and Jim opened their B&B, (my old infant's school), especially for my son Craig and I. I am grateful to them for making it an excellent and informative stay.

What can I say to my son Craig for his superb talent? He exceeded my expectations in his illustrations.

Just in case they think I have forgotten them, thank you also to my sons Alex and Lewis for their encouraging words after reading about my childhood.

Finally, to Mac, who so patiently read and re-read the manuscript. At each "tut-tut" and "dear oh dear", of which there were many, I knew he would be correcting my grammar and punctuation. Thank you dear, dear husband, your "tuts" have helped make a much-improved product.

# Afterword

This afterword provides some detail as to what became of the members of my family and the other people who enriched my childhood, in the time since the end of the memoir. Other than my family, I lost touch with many of those people and have tried, mostly unsuccessfully, to locate them either through social media or by revisiting the north east. At the time of writing I am sixty-six years old and unsurprisingly, most of the adults in my childhood have since died.

## My Family

After moving from Northumberland in 1964 we lived with the Collinses in Clacton-on-Sea for nine months - until my parents had the means to buy their own property. It was a trying time for the adults and tested their friendship. However, we all survived and I know Mum and Dad were entirely grateful to the Collins family for giving us a home for so long.

**Mum and Dad** lived and worked in and around the Clacton area. Dad worked as a labourer on various sites: building the sea wall at Jaywick Sands, or on housing projects across the county. In his final years of working, when he became too old for labouring, he took on the steward's role in the Comrades Club in Clacton – a working-man's club. This was quite a departure for him but he settled into the job as if he should have been doing it all his life. He and Mum made a lot of friends through the club. Meanwhile Mum worked during the summer months in seasonal jobs in Butlins Holiday camp and amusement arcades. For a short time she also worked as an auxiliary nurse in the Clacton rehabilitation centre. She did not take on any full time jobs as Sally and Michael were still at school.

Dad retired in 1983 at the age of sixty-five. Mum had been telling him for several years that as soon as he reached retirement they would return to Malin Head to live. She said she had waited over forty years to go home and that if he didn't want to go with her she would go without him. He went of course. They built a small bungalow in Killourt, overlooking White Strand bay, twenty-five yards from the house Kath and Bob had built a few years earlier. Mum was home at last, "to her dying day" she said. Dad filled his time building a kitchen, a turf shed and other jobs that needed doing. He enjoyed his Guinness at the pub with his old friends. Mum relished being close to her sisters and they took up where they had left off forty years previously.

Life was good for the first year but then Dad suffered an aneurism, which put him in intensive care fighting for his life. The aneurism was repaired but due to complications his kidneys became irreparably damaged. He survived another four years and lived as enjoyable a life as he was able. He died at the age of seventy in his home in July 1989.

Mum adapted to life without her husband. She loved her garden and despite the windy, salt-laden air of Malin Head she managed to grow flowers along the garden walls that surrounded her bungalow. She lived comfortably on her own for a number of years but after a couple of hip replacements in her eighties her health began to suffer. My sister Sally moved in and lived with her as her carer for the last eight years of her life. Mum died peacefully at the age of ninety-one in her home in July 2013, her wish granted.

**Hubert**, (who became known as Hugh) and his first wife divorced while he was in the Royal Navy. He left the service after nine years and became a successful salesman, initially selling insurance and later, welding rods. He married Brenda in April 1978 and they had a son and daughter. They lived in the Southampton area while the children were growing up. When Hugh was sixty-two, he developed bowel cancer and was forced to give up his job. He and Brenda moved to Spain in the hope the warm climate would aid his recovery. At one stage he was declared cancer free but it returned and spread to his liver. After several painful operations and bouts of chemotherapy he died in hospital five years later in 2010. He was sixty-nine.

**Kathleen**, (who became known as Kath) continued her nursing career for many years. During that time she met and married Bob and lived in Sale, Manchester. They had a daughter and son. Kath suffered a significant back injury while nursing, caused by lifting heavy patients from their beds. In those days the nurses did not have the aid of bed hoists. Kath gave up nursing and in the late 1970's the family moved to Malin Head and built a seven bedroomed house in Killourt overlooking White Strand Bay. They set up a Bed & Breakfast business and entertained many visitors from all over the world. At the same time they opened a fish and chip shop and worked long hours running both businesses. After four years they closed the fish and chip shop and Kath became involved in promoting tourism in the area. She helped organise the opening of a 'typical Irish cottage' for tourists to visit. She then took a job working for the Northern Ireland North and West housing project, which came under the auspices of the medical authority. Her responsibility involved setting up homes in Derry/ Londonderry to house patients with mental and physical difficulties, whose symptoms were not severe enough to require hospitalisation. She helped them settle back into the community. She stayed in this job for fifteen years. During that time Kath suffered a further serious back injury in a driving accident. She underwent a major operation to insert a metal plate and screws in her spine: this severely impaired her mobility. She was forced to take disability retirement in 1999. Kath and Bob retired to the Alicante area in Spain in 2001 where they still live. Kath is now seventy-three.

Joe spent a few years serving in Trinity House during which time he earned his Master's Ticket and reached the rank of First Mate. He met and married Margaret in 1974. They had two children, a daughter and a son. After Joe left Trinity House his career took many twists and turns. He tested his entrepreneurial skills in the Nottingham area buying and selling used cars. When he had done with cars he bought and sold used pleasure boats and yachts. He and his wife returned to Ireland and set up house in Moville - a coastal town on the Inishowen Peninsular, Co Donegal. He had made enough money to buy a large bungalow on the scenic eastern shore of Loch Foyle, about forty minutes drive south east of Malin Head. Here Joe bought a small boat and contracted with the authorities to deliver pilots to ships bound for Londonderry port. After a few years he sold the boat and leased a pub in Moville. A couple of years of pub life was quite enough. Joe took on refrigeration unit repairs for supermarkets. He and Margaret bought a house in Eglington on the outskirts of Derry/Londonderry, which is still the family home. During these years they also bought two properties in Spain in the Alicante region, one for personal use, the other for holiday lets.

In 2008, at the age of sixty-three Joe began to show signs of dementia. Sadly, in 2010, he was diagnosed with the most aggressive form of Alzheimer's Disease. The condition progressed to the stage where he no longer recognises any of his brothers and sisters. He is seventy-two and currently lives in a care home in Derry/Londonderry and seems to be happy.

**John** could not settle to life in Clacton-on-Sea. He was fifteen when we moved south. He spent the summer months working in Butlins Holiday Camp before deciding to return to Northumberland. His ambition had always been to ride horses and he secured a job with the Arthur Stevenson stables - initially as a stable boy but eventually progressing to become a steeplechase jockey. During that time he met and married Lesley. They had one daughter. John's life as a jockey met with limited success. He won a few races but mostly he finished in the mix. His career was beset with injury – he broke his femur, which required pins to set it. He also broke his back and was in a brace for six weeks. Eventually his injuries put an end to his horseracing. He worked as a logistics manager for a large haulage company in the Rotherham area, South Yorkshire. In the early 2000's he and his wife again returned to the northeast. They bought a Bed & Breakfast business in the seaside village of Bamburgh, about ten miles south of Berwick-on-Tweed and not far from where these memoirs are set. They sold that business five years later and bought a bungalow in Belford, the village where he and I attended secondary school. He took up work for a market gardener as well as driving children from the outer regions to and from school. John is sixty-seven and semi-retired. He and Lesley remain in Belford and he still chauffeurs the schoolchildren.

**Sally** grew up in Clacton. At the age of sixteen she left school and attended a two-year drama course at Colchester technical college. After a few years of unsatisfactory jobs she moved to Malin Head and lived with Kath and Bob. She helped run the B&B and also helped set up and run the fish and chip shop. Later she worked in the Irish cottage, baked scones and greeted tourists. She opened a beauty salon in Carndonnagh in 1988, a small town eight miles south of Malin Head. At the age of thirty Sally gave birth to a daughter. She had been in a long-term relationship with a local man but they had split up before the baby was born. When her baby was a year old she took an Art & Design course at the University of Ulster. During this time she met Jurgen, a German tourist. They corresponded and he came back to visit Sally on several occasions. When she completed the Design course she moved with her daughter to Germany to live with Jurgen. Nine years later, and fluent in German, Sally and her daughter returned to live in Carndonnagh. Her German language skills helped her secure part-time work in the local tourist office. At the same time she gave part-time care to Mum who was becoming more infirm with hip pain. When Mum became housebound and could no longer look after herself, Sally gave up her job to become her full-time carer. After Mum died Sally took up work again at the tourist office where she continues to welcome visitors. She is fifty-eight and still lives in Mum and Dad's bungalow.

**Michael** (who became known as Mike) also grew up in Clacton and lives there still. He had no interest in further education and left school at sixteen. He took up a dental technician apprenticeship making dental appliances for East Essex Dental Laboratory. He met and married Val in 1991. The young couple took a break from work and travelled around Australia for a year in a camper van. They also spent a few months touring America. When travelling was well and truly out of their system they settled in a bungalow in Clacton, near the sea front. During this time they had two daughters. The bungalow needed modernisation and, to save money, Mike spent many years making the renovations. He knocked out and rebuilt walls, built a conservatory, installed a new bathroom and kitchen, and much, much more. Until recently Mike contracted with a private company called Medicar. He was responsible for driving patients, who did not require an ambulance but who were unable to drive themselves, to and from their homes to NHS hospital appointments. He continues to work as a dental technician but on a part-time basis. Mike is fifty-five years old.

## Hetton Hall Residents

**The Fiddeses** - Big John and Jesse Fiddes lived in Hetton Hall through the seventies and eighties. In the late eighties, they bought a smallholding five miles from Hetton Hall. Here they lived a self-sufficient life working the small amount of land they owned. In 1999 Jesse became ill at the age of 72 and died in the same year. Big John, a year younger than Jesse, had been devoted to her all his married life and died a few months later. June, their daughter, told me that he could not cope with the loneliness.

June attended teacher's training college and became a secondary school teacher. We lost touch for many years but in 2010 I made contact with her again through social media. She married and had three children. Her first husband died suddenly of a brain tumor. The shock sent her into a gloom - life became difficult. With the support and help from her children she gradually emerged from her loss. She met and married another man and she now lives in the Costa Blanca region of Spain with her husband.

Little John, the middle child, lived with his parents. He worked on the land until he married and moved to Lowick. Much later he set up his own business dealing with farm feed supplies. I believe he still runs this business with his brother Ashley.

**The Thompsons** - I met Mr and Mrs Thompson once more in 1980 when I took my husband Mac and three children to the northeast for a holiday. I was keen to show Mac and my children where I grew up. Mrs Thompson still wore her hair, now grey, in a bun. Mr Thompson looked older but his gentle countenance remained. They moved from the

Big House to a smaller place in Berwick-on-Tweed some years after we left Hetton Hall. By this time all their children had left home. I have no information on the three elder daughters but I had heard that Mark attended boarding school and then attended university. He moved to South Africa. Mr and Mrs Thompson both died some time in the 2000's.

**The Collinses** - Rose and Big James Collins lived and work in Clacton until they retired to Malin Head in the early 1980's. Big James died soon after.

Rosemary attended university in London and studied psychology. She worked for the Social Services, which later became the Department of Work and Pensions. She married and had three sons.

Evelyn attended teachers training college in London and became an infant teacher. She married and lived temporarily with her husband in Persia (later Iran) They returned to England after two years and settled in Chester. They had four daughters.

James and Anthony did not pursue further education. Both found local jobs and eventually moved to London.

Patricia worked as an IT consultant.

Apart from Patricia the tale of the Collins children is a sad one. Three died early deaths due to illness. Evelyn died in 1996 at the age of forty-eight. James and Anthony died a few years apart in the early 2000's, each in their forties. Rosemary died from lung cancer in 2008 at the age of fifty-nine.

Patricia is retired and currently lives in Marks Tey, Essex with her partner.

Rose and Mum continued their friendship in Malin Head, a friendship that lasted over sixty years. Each time I came to visit my parents I called on Rose and listened again to snippets from her bag of stories. She published a small book of poems, some of which have been set to music by the daughter of a friend in Malin Head. Rose lived a long life and died in 2012 at the age of eighty-five.

**As for me**, I desperately wanted to move into further education. My ambition was to become an English and Sports teacher. Dad was adamant that I leave school, get a job and bring money into the household. "What's the point of her staying on? She'll only get married and have children." Our relationship throughout my teenage years remained frosty and I was convinced he refused to let me pursue education out of spite. I found a job with a chemical company called Bexford that manufactured photographic film-base. The company was later taken over by ICI. I worked in the laboratories as a lab technician carrying out various tests on the properties of the product. I enjoyed the job and learnt a lot. I was earning money, although the majority of it went into my mother's purse for my board and lodgings. It was in the labs that I met my husband Mac in October 1969. He arrived fresh from university as a young graduate and it wasn't long before we were dating. Nine months later we married in September 1970. "It'll never last," they all said, "whirlwind romances never do." (Forty-seven years later, we are still together.) Alex, our first son was born two years after we married. Our twin sons, Craig and Lewis, were born on Christmas Eve two years after that – what a shock when I discovered a week before due date that they were a pair.

I left work to look after my children. Dad was right after all.

Mac resigned from ICI and became a Physics teacher, first in Birmingham and subsequently in Sherborne, Dorset, where we lived for nine years. When the boys attended school full-time I found a part-time job, six hours a week, in a tiny public library in Castle Cary, which eventually led to a full-time role in Sherborne library. When the boys were of secondary school age we moved back to the Midlands. For two years I worked in a dull administrative job in the computing department of British Gas in Solihull until, at the age of thirty-nine, I took and passed their computing aptitude test. From there my career leapt forward. Over subsequent years I worked for a large American company mainly on Government projects. Mac left education and joined the same company. The advantage of us working together in similar roles meant we could take up opportunities in places such as Lytham-St-Annes in Lancashire, Tynemouth in Newcastle and more exotically, Sydney in Australia.

We both retired in 2010. I took up golf and tap dancing. I also joined a number of U3A (University of the Third Age) groups, in particular Creative Writing. It is this group that inspired me to write these memoirs.